THE KEW BOOK *of* EMBROIDERED FLOWERS

TRISH BURR

DEDICATION
For all lovers of botanical art.

THE KEW BOOK of
EMBROIDERED
FLOWERS

TRISH BURR

SEARCH PRESS

'He has made everything beautiful in his time.'
Ecclesiastes 3:11

First published in 2020

Search Press Limited
Wellwood, North Farm Road,
Tunbridge Wells, Kent TN2 3DR

Text © Trish Burr 2020
Photographs by Stacey Burr

With special thanks to Rachel Pedder-Smith for permission to reproduce her Magenta Flower Line painting in stitch, shown on pages 36–37 and 44–93, and to the Natural History Museum: the *Geranium phaeum* illustration by Arthur Harry Church was reproduced in stitch and shown on pages 14, 17, 18, 19, 20 and 34.

Photographs and design © Search Press Ltd. 2020

Folder edition with transfers ISBN: 978-1-78221-642-1
Hardback edition ISBN: 978-1-78221-906-4

Please note, iron-on transfers are only available with the folder edition of this title.

Suppliers
If you have any difficulty obtaining any of the materials and equipment mentioned in this book, please visit the Search Press website:
www.searchpress.com

Visit Trish's website:
www.trishbembroidery.com

ACKNOWLEDGEMENTS

'Feeling gratitude and not expressing it is like wrapping a present and not giving it.'
– William Arthur Ward

I would like to thank all those involved in the creation of this book, in particular Katie French and Becky Robbins from Search Press, and Gina Fullerlove from Kew Gardens, who were instrumental in its conception – thank you for allowing me the privilege of reproducing such beautiful botanical works of art in embroidery. To my editor, Becky, who is always kind and cheerful – thank you for your patience, advice and guidance throughout the process.

To Betsy Hosegood, for your meticulous editing of the instructions for the book – you managed to make sense of it all and I now know that 'a grasshopper does not have a tail'! To Rachel Pedder-Smith for allowing me the use of your beautiful Magenta Flower Line painting, and to Nathalie and Marc at Au Ver À Soie for donating the full range of their exquisite silk Soie d'Alger for use in this book – lucky me! To Pei Chu, the publishing assistant at Kew, who has kindly assisted with sources of botanical illustration. To my daughter Stacey in London, who shot all the beautiful photographs for this book; there is no one else who could capture the essence of my embroidery through the lens of a camera quite like you, and I love that we got to share this experience.

On a more personal note: to my youngest daughter, Katie, on whom I rely for advice on colours, composition and help with my embroidery – thank you for watching The Bachelor with me and for keeping us current in the world of K-Pop bands and Korean drama! To Tess, I am so proud of the person you have become, – you are a great listener and motivator; thank you for being my inspiration. To my long-suffering husband, Simon – thank you for patiently pretending to listen and be interested in my embroidery when you would rather be watching the rugby! I am so grateful to have you in my life. To Mum and Dad, thank you for your love, guidance and support.

Last but not least, thanks to my customers, students and readers who support my efforts, forgive my mistakes and never allow me to rest on my laurels – I hope you love this book: these pages are for you.

CONTENTS

Foreword	6
Introduction	8
What is needle painting?	10
Tools and materials	10
Preparation	16
Stitch instructions	20
Outlines	30
Raised embroidery	32
Anatomy of a flower	34
Useful advice before you start	35

Simple projects	36
Starter project: Japanese anemone	38
Flower sampler	44
Clematis	94
Camellia	100
Intermediate projects	106
Rhododendron	108
Waterlily	116
Iris	122
Spider chrysanthemum	128
Advanced projects	134
Rose	136
Magnolia	144
Poppy sampler	154
Thread substitutes	163
The templates	164
Using iron-on transfers	176

'People from a planet without flowers would think we must be mad with joy the whole time to have such things about us.' – Iris Murdoch

Papaversomniferum L.

T BURR 17

FOREWORD

Kew's Library, Art & Archives was established in the mid-1850s and now forms one of the greatest collections of botanical information to be found anywhere. The collection supports the work of Kew's scientists and horticulturists but is also accessed by thousands of researchers, garden enthusiasts, historians and the general public around the world. Visits in person to the collection are warmly encouraged.

The botanical illustration collection is a world-renowned resource – the largest of its kind – assembled over the last 200 years and containing some 200,000 pieces ranging in date from the 18th century to the present day. The illustrations form an exceptional visual record of the diversity of the plant and fungal kingdoms and have historical value in terms of provenance, context and in relation to specific plant hunters.

While visually stunning, the illustrations are a working collection: they are an important scientific tool in the process of taxonomy – the identifying and naming of plants and fungi. The purpose of the illustration is to enable the species to be identified, so accuracy is essential in documenting the visual characteristics of the plant or fungus. All the features of the species are included; its seeds, flowers, fruits etc., arranged in an artistically appealing way – something which may not be possible with photography.

Kew's collection contains works by the greatest names in botanical illustration, including paintings by the great 18th-century masters such as Georg Dionysius Ehret, Pierre-Joseph Redouté, and Franz and Ferdinand Bauer, through to Walter Hood Fitch in the 19th century, and the work of contemporary illustrators contributing to publications such as *Curtis's Botanical Magazine* and *Kew Bulletin*.

Works range in media and dimension, from pocket-sized sketchbooks to large-format pieces measuring up to 3m (10ft) in width. In addition, the collection contains a large number of portraits of eminent scientists, botanical artists and explorers, spanning several centuries to the current day, and a collection of photographs which record plants, their uses, and the history of Kew.

But the illustrations are, of course, also a wonderful resource for artistic inspiration and have been reinterpreted by other artists and craftspeople in new and exiting ways. Trish Burr's delicate and beautiful embroidery presents another way of looking at Kew's illustrations, bringing out the colours and giving the images a three-dimensional quality, both reflecting and enhancing the originals on which they are based and encouraging us to look at them afresh.

Fiona Ainsworth
Head of Library, Art & Archives
Royal Botanic Gardens, Kew

INTRODUCTION

'The real voyage of discovery consists not in seeking new landscapes, but in having new eyes.' – Marcel Proust

I grew up on a farm with my family, enveloped in a large farming community. I was a shy child, preferring tree-climbing and bike-riding to the company of others, but I loved to draw and would pick flowers from my Mum's garden and spend hours painting them in watercolour. I did do needlework lessons at school, but I had no interest in them. My skills must have been sadly lacking, as the teacher merely wrote in my school report: 'Patricia tries'! Although I loved art there was no expectation of making it into a career – it was simply accepted in those days that I would go to secretarial college, get a job, hopefully meet a man and get married. Happily for me this is what happened, and my husband of 37 years and I now have three gorgeous grown-up girls who are all creative in their own ways. But at the age of 40, I became interested in embroidery and my life shifted in a whole new direction.

My embroidery career so far has provided many wonderful, surprising opportunities that I would never have dreamed possible. But perhaps one of the most thrilling has been the invitation to reproduce the beautiful botanical illustrations of the Royal Botanic Gardens, Kew in embroidery. For me, this is no ordinary embroidery book, for it has combined my love of botanical art with my love of embroidery. It has been a delightful journey of discovery – I have gained a new appreciation for the explorers behind the art, the legacy they have left behind and for the incredible Kew Organisation as a whole.

This book is about botanical art in needle painting. If you are familiar with my work, you will know that I am self-taught so have developed my own style of needle painting, and it has been my experience that anyone can learn this style of embroidery. If you are a beginner, please don't be nervous about having a go – it is not difficult and with a little practice you will soon be up and away! It is important to allow a certain degree of self-expression, and not be your own worst critic. Embroidery is individual, so if your work does not look exactly like mine or your neighbour's, that's okay! As long as it is pleasing to you, it is a success – I hope this gives you the freedom to enjoy your embroidery and not stress about how it *should* look.

The projects in this book cater for all levels of expertise, from beginner to advanced. If you are new to embroidery you could begin with the practice shapes and the starter sampler, but if you feel so inclined, why not dive straight in and try one of the simple projects – you will be amazed to find that you have unleashed a creative side that you never knew you had! On the other hand, I am sure that all you more experienced stitchers will relish the prospect of working on something as beautiful and enduring as the botanical illustrations from the Kew Art Collection.

If you find that the information in this book differs slightly from any of my previous books, this is because I am always learning new and improved ways of doing things and finding better materials to work with. I hope the projects inspire and motivate you to grow in your love of needle painting, and that your stitching will give you and others much pleasure for generations to come.

Remember to smile while you stitch: it prevents wrinkles and calms the mind.

Enjoy the journey and happy stitching!

WHAT IS NEEDLE PAINTING?

Needle painting is a surface embroidery technique – it is like painting a picture on fabric with a needle and thread. An outline of the image is first traced and transferred on to the fabric, then filled with embroidery using the original image as a reference. Needle painting is also referred to as silk shading, long-and-short shading or thread painting – these are just different names for the same technique. The main stitch used for needle painting is long-and-short stitch, which is normally done in one strand of cotton or silk thread. Long-and-short stitch allows you to fill an area with subtle blends of colour, which results in the realistic 'painted' finish and the beautiful shading for which it is renowned.

Of course, a few other stitches are also needed to mimic specific areas in the picture. Since we are principally concerned with botanical subjects in this book, each part of a plant will be stitched using the appropriate stitch to make it look most lifelike. We will discuss this in more depth in the section on Stitch Instructions (see pages 20–29).

TOOLS AND MATERIALS

FABRICS

Pure natural fibres such as 100 per cent linen, cotton or silk are ideal for needle painting embroidery. Generally, the fabric you use should be very closely woven to allow for the precise placement of each stitch and have very little stretch in it to prevent distortion when mounted into the hoop. Although I prefer to use quite specific fabrics for needle painting, there are many other fabrics that could be used and I don't want to limit you, so here are some features to look for when purchasing your own fabric:

- **Good quality:** always use the best quality fabric you can afford. Beware of cheap imitations as they may look fine, but once the embroidery is complete they may cause puckering or distortion and cause all sorts of problems.

- **Pure fibres:** where possible, use pure natural fibres such as cotton, linen and silk; avoid synthetic fibres.

- **Close weave:** make sure the fabric has a very tight, close weave; generally, if it is a heavy fabric, it will have a looser weave. Avoid gauzy, translucent, flimsy, soft or floppy fabrics – you want fabric with a bit of body so it will support the embroidery. If in doubt, look in the quilting section for good-quality cottons.

- **The stretch test:** make sure the fabric has little or no stretch in it – if the fabric is stretchy, it will distort in the hoop and cause major puckering. Do the 'stretch test': pull and stretch the fabric along both sides along the grain – if it stretches a lot, it is not suitable. You want the fabric to be quite crisp. If in doubt, purchase several samples and try them out at home before using.

- **Not suitable:** evenweave linens for counted thread embroidery or cross stitch are not suitable. The weave will be too loose, and you will not have enough placement for your needle.

LINEN

Linen is my fabric of choice. The linen you use for needle painting should have a very high thread count, be of medium weight to support the stitching and a very tight, smooth weave. Linens with a loose weave, textured linens or linens for dressmaking are not suitable.

PROS: linen is very resilient and a joy to work on as the fibres will spring back into shape when washed or ironed. It is a strong, robust fabric that does not mark easily and, for some reason, iron-on transfers seem to work better on linen than cotton, giving a clear and strong print.

CONS: fine-quality linen that was produced in the past for use in bedsheets and tablecloths – the type of linen used by our grandmothers for embroidery – is no longer produced due to a lack of demand in the commercial world. It is only available from specialist outlets, and is therefore expensive and can be difficult to obtain.

NB: at the time of going to press I have a premium, Belgian linen fabric available for sale in my online store. The closest alternative (but not as fine) is an Irish linen or church linen, which can be ordered from online church suppliers.

COTTON

A good-quality cotton muslin (also known as calico), such as that used for heirloom embroidery and quilting, can be successfully used for needle painting. It should be at least 200 count and evenly woven across the weft and warp to prevent distortion in the hoop. Cotton satin also works well, as, despite its name, it is a pure cotton fabric – the term satin describes the weave. Other cotton fabrics such as denim or poplin that are medium weight and have a very close, smooth weave could also be used – make sure they are pure cotton, not mixed, and have no stretch in them.

PROS: cotton muslin is easy to source, less expensive than linen and provides a nice smooth, tight weave for needle painting. It is a good fabric to start with for beginners in embroidery.

CONS: cotton is not as strong and durable as linen and may distort and mark more easily. Iron-on transfers will work well on cotton but the print will not be as defined as it is on linen.

NB: at the time of going to press, superior-quality 200 count cotton muslin is available for sale in my online store. If you are desperate and don't want to wait for shipping, purchase a good-quality 200 count (or higher) bed sheet or pillowcase, which can be cut up and used for stitching. Don't forget to do the stretch test first.

SILK AND SATIN

A good-quality natural silk dupion can also be used for needle painting. The silk should preferably be the powerwoven kind (not handwoven) so that it has fewer slubs and a nice smooth finish. It should be a medium weight and 100 per cent pure silk, not mixed or synthetic. Other silk and satin fabrics such as good-quality silk tafetta or pure silk duchesse satin can also be used successfully.

PROS: silk is divine to stitch on as the needle glides through the fibres with no resistance. It comes in a large selection of colours and has good body with a very tight weave, which provides a supportive ground fabric for needle painting.

CONS: silk marks easily, as I have found out! You need to be mindful of stains while stitching as it is difficult to remove the marks and great care needs to be taken when washing silk fabric. Good-quality, pure silk fabrics are expensive, and will need to be purchased from a specialist shop or outlet, preferably one that supplies wedding fabrics.

NB: you cannot use iron-on transfers on silk – you will have to transfer design outlines by hand.

BACKING FABRIC

If you are using a medium-weight, close weave fabric that is sturdy enough to support the stitching, it is not necessary to use a backing fabric. I prefer not to use one but the choice is yours. If you do decide to use a backing fabric, choose a fine cotton muslin or similar.

PROS: backing fabric can provide extra support if your ground fabric is too thin or flimsy. If your ground fabric has a loose or rough weave, a backing fabric can create a smoother consistency to stitch on.

CONS: it is difficult to line up the main and backing fabrics correctly, which can result in puckering when removed from the frame or hoop. When mounting your embroidery, you will need to stretch and mount the backing and ground fabrics separately to achieve a good result.

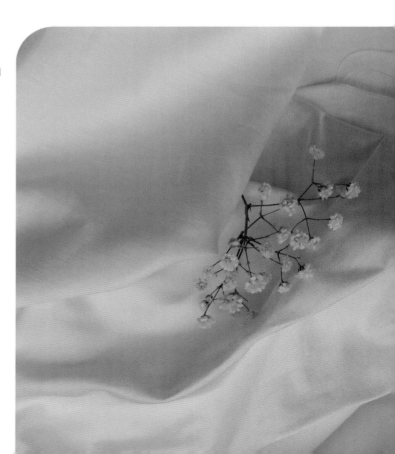

THREADS

DMC or Anchor stranded cotton and Au Ver À Soie, Soie d'Alger silks are used for the projects in this book. Stranded cotton is readily available from online needlework stores or your local high street store in most countries. Many needlework stores carry the full range of Soie D'Alger, but if you are unable to get hold of them you can use the conversion chart provided on page 163, which will give you the closest match to DMC stranded cotton. Please be aware that it is not possible to provide exact colour matches, so if you choose to use substitutes your embroidery will look different to the original.

A rainbow of DMC stranded cotton threads.

STRANDED COTTON (OR FLOSS)

DMC stranded cotton is the most commonly used brand of stranded cotton. It offers a huge variety of colours and lends itself perfectly to needle painting. Cotton thread is easy to use, durable, colourfast, washable and can resist exposure to light. DMC threads are made from the best long-staple cotton in the world and mercerized twice to give an exceptional sheen. The thread is comprised of six easily separated strands, and you will normally use one strand in your embroidery, unless otherwise directed. Anchor is another brand of good-quality stranded cotton that can be used together or alternatively with DMC. If you choose to use any other brand, be sure that it is colourfast and good quality.

A selection of Au Ver À Soie threads.

HOW TO USE COTTON OR SILK THREAD

Pull out a length of thread from the skein of about 50–60cm (20–24in). Separate one strand. Cut this off and thread into the needle. Use one strand of thread throughout unless otherwise instructed in the pattern.

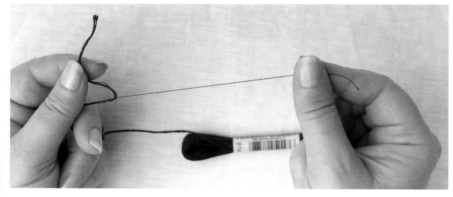

THREAD NAP

All thread has a 'nap' – this is the direction in which the pile of the yarn lies. It helps to achieve smoother stitching if you thread the yarn in the same direction each time, as this allows the nap to remain in the same direction while stitching.

SOIE D'ALGER SILK

This is a luxurious, supreme-quality silk thread from Paris, France. It is my silk thread of choice as it has a moderate lustre, which lends itself perfectly to the natural look we want to achieve in our needle painting. Soie D'Alger is easy to use and does not stick to your fingers or get tangled while stitching. It is made of the best quality spun silk (called *strusas*), which gives it an unrivalled regularity, lustrousness and softness. One strand of Soie D'Alger is slightly thicker than one strand of DMC cotton, but they can be successfully used together, or alternately, for stitching. The thread is comprised of seven easily separated strands, and you would normally use one strand in your embroidery unless otherwise directed. Silk thread is not always colourfast, so it is recommended that you consider dry cleaning your embroidery if cleaning is necessary, or you can steam clean it as outlined on page 18.

A selection of polyester machine threads, which are sometimes needed for outlining.

POLYESTER SEWING THREAD FOR OUTLINES

One strand of stranded cotton can normally be used for outlining, but sometimes even this is too thick and you may need a more delicate outline for specific areas. When required, you can split one strand of polyester sewing cotton into two and use one of these very fine threads for outlining. To split polyester sewing thread, cut a length and tease open the ends with the blunt end of a needle – you will see that it can easily be separated into two. Simply pull the strands apart, separate one, and thread it into your needle.

Any good-quality sewing thread can be used. Some silk threads, such as Soie De Paris, can also be split and used for outlines. Simply match up the nearest shade of sewing or silk thread to the outline thread shade given in the pattern.

HOOPS AND FRAMES

SUPER GRIP HOOP (1)

The best type of hoop to use for surface embroidery is a super grip hoop such as a Susan Bates Hoop-La™ or similar. This hoop will grip your fabric and keep it absolutely drum-tight, which is necessary to prevent puckering of your embroidery. These hoops can be purchased online or from any good needlework store.

PROS: quick and simple to use, these keep your fabric drum-tight. You can easily adjust your tension while stitching.

CONS: they can leave a hoop mark that is difficult to remove. To prevent this you will need to bind the hoop and make a hoop cover (see page 16).

STRETCHER FRAME (2)

Stretcher bars come in pairs of different lengths so you can connect them together to make the size you want. They should be very light and as thin as possible, so that they are easy to hold in the hand. Brands such as Siesta Frames in the UK and Edmunds in the US are ideal because they are very lightweight, but any similar stretcher bars will do. If you can't find these, you can buy a lightweight artists' canvas frame from an art shop and remove the canvas.

PROS: does not leave a hoop mark. Can be assembled to fit the size of the embroidery and keeps embroidery fabric aligned with the grain of the fabric. Does not require a hoop cover or binding on the frame.

CONS: a little extra preparation is required to stretch and insert thumb tacks. Thumb tacks need to be removed to adjust the tension.

THUMB TACKS

You will need thumb tacks to secure the fabric to the stretcher frame. The steel ones with a flat top are ideal, but you can also buy a thumb tack kit, which includes a magnetic tool to push the tacks in and a tack extractor – these save a lot of wear and tear on your fingers!

NEEDLES (3)

You will need a sharps needle (also known as a general sewing needle) for needle painting. It has a round eye and short shaft, which allows for the stabbing motion you use in needle painting and is easier to control when creating smaller stitches. Sizes range from 2–12: the larger the number, the smaller the needle. You should use sharps numbers 10–11 for one strand of thread, and sharps numbers 9–10 for two strands of thread.

If you find it difficult to see the eye of the needle, you could also use a crewel embroidery needle with a longer eye in sizes 9–11. Crewel embroidery needles can be useful if using more than one strand of thread in specific circumstances.

I like Bohin needles because they go through the fabric like a hot knife through butter and do not tarnish or bend, but any good brand of needle such as John James, Richard Hemming or Clover can be used. It is recommended that you dispose of your needle when it starts to tarnish and use a new needle for each project so that it does not damage your thread or fabric.

SCISSORS (4)

You will need a small sharp pair of embroidery scissors. I like the Kai curved scissors, as they cut cleanly and sharply and are good for unpicking too, but any good-quality embroidery scissors will do.

daylight™

A magnifying light will make detailed stitching and colour placement much easier to achieve.

MAGNIFYING LIGHT

This is one of the most important tools for this style of embroidery and will be the best investment you ever make! It is virtually impossible for you to see the fine stitches in your needle painting without one. The belief that simply magnifying your work makes it easier to see is not true – sitting in a badly lit area and trying to magnify a dark image will not help. What makes your work easier to see is light – the combination of bright light and magnification is ideal and will reduce eye strain while stitching. You need a magnifying light that has daylight or white light equivalent so that it does not distort the colours you are working with.

WHICH MAGNIFYING LIGHT?

I often get asked this question as there are many magnifying lights on the market to choose from. I would recommend that you get the best you can afford. I have tried many lights, some more expensive than others, but I now use the Daylight Slimline LED Magnifying Lamp with a 13-cm (5-in) glass and 21 LEDS (see above). The new LED lights are great – they provide a bright, white light so there are no shadows on your work and the bulbs do not need replacing. I like to sit comfortably in my armchair while stitching, so I have a light on a floor stand that I can adjust to my needs, but you could use either a table clamp, desktop or floor stand – whatever you feel most comfortable with. Any good online craft/needlework store is a good place to find a variety of magnifying lamps to suit your pocket and preference.

If for any reason you are unable to use a magnifying light, ensure that you work under a bright light and consider using reading spectacles for magnifying your work. These come in different magnifications, so find the ones that suit you. If you already use spectacles, the reading spectacles can be placed on top of your regular spectacles to magnify the viewing area.

PREPARATION

PREPARING YOUR FABRIC

- Wash and iron your fabric to remove creases and pre-shrink it. It is not advisable to wash silk or satin, but both can be pressed lightly with an iron (not a steam iron).
- Line up the grain – to do this, pull a thread on two sides at right angles to ensure that it is on the straight grain.
- Overcast the edges of the fabric with a sewing machine, or use masking tape, a glue stick or fray-stop to prevent fraying.

TRANSFERRING THE OUTLINE BY HAND

To transfer a design outline manually using the templates on pages 164–175, here is a simple method:

- Trace the outline onto a piece of tracing paper or have it photocopied.
- Place the outline onto a lightbox or on a window and secure with masking tape.
- Place your fabric centrally on top of this and again tape in place.
- With the light showing through you will easily be able to see the lines – trace over these lines with an HB pencil or a fine micron pen size 005.

For advice on using iron-on transfers, see page 176.

PREPARING A HOOP

BIND THE HOOP

To prevent damage to your fabric, bind the inner hoop with strips of white or off-white fabric. You can use fabric glue to secure the end and prevent unravelling.

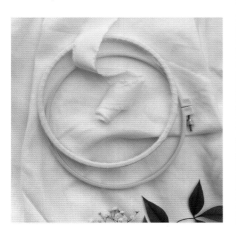

HOOP COVER

To prevent hoop marks on your fabric while stitching, make a hoop cover:

- Cut a piece of scrap fabric. It is best to use white or off-white.
- Cut a small hole in the centre of the fabric.
- Place your embroidery fabric over the inner hoop and the scrap fabric on top of this.
- Centre the design in the hoop.
- Cut away the excess fabric to reveal your design, as shown.

MOUNTING YOUR FABRIC IN A HOOP

- Both pieces of fabric – main and cover – need to be mounted into the hoop together, so place both fabrics over the inner hoop, lip facing up.
- Place the outer hoop over this.
- Push it down and you will feel the outer hoop slip under the lip of the inner hoop.
- Tighten the screw and stretch the fabric, then repeat this until the fabric is drum-tight. The fabric needs to be very taut to provide a good tension.
- Stretch the fabric on the straight grain, across and down as shown. Do not stretch on the bias, as the fabric will overstretch and result in distortion when removed.

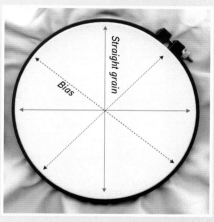

Here the straight grain is shown with red arrows; the bias is shown with blue arrows.

MOUNTING YOUR FABRIC IN A FRAME

- Place the fabric face down on a table (the embroidery outline will be facing down).
- Place the frame on top of this (on the back of the fabric). Ensure that the outline is centred within the frame.
- Pull the fabric on each side over the bars and secure with tacks, easing the fabric into place so that it is very taut.
- Adjust the fabric as necessary until it is tightly stretched across the frame.

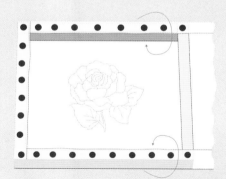
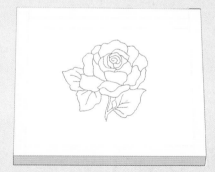

The back of the emboidery, mounted in a frame.

WASHING YOUR EMBROIDERY

- Soak your embroidery in warm water using a mild soap (I use an organic castile soap).
- Rinse thoroughly in cold water.
- Wrap in a fluffy towel to remove excess moisture.
- Place face down on a towel and either block (see below) or leave to dry.

Please note that if you have used silk thread, it is not advisable to wash your embroidery as the colours tend to run – you will have to dry clean it or steam as outlined for blocking, below.

BLOCKING YOUR EMBROIDERY

There may be times when your completed stitching is badly puckered or distorted, or there is a stubborn hoop mark that is hard to remove. Blocking your embroidery is an easy way to freshen and restore it to its original shape. If DMC stranded cotton has been used for the embroidery, it can be washed and then blocked, but if silk threads have been used, it is not advisable to wash it, but it can be blocked using the method below. All you need is a cork or polystyrene board and some map pins.

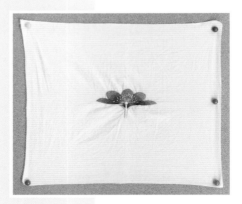

COTTON THREAD METHOD
- Wash your embroidery as outlined above.
- Place the damp fabric on a surface such as cork or foam – make sure it has a straight edge.
- Line up your embroidery on the straight edge on one side and place pins at each corner, then pin all along the first edge.
- Do the same on the other three sides – stretch the fabric as you go and move your corner pins if you need to. Ensure that the fabric is stretched tight with no creases.
- Leave until completely dry or use a hairdryer if you are in a hurry.
- Remove the pins and, if necessary, press lightly with a hot iron on the wrong side.

SILK THREAD METHOD
- Stretch the embroidery onto a cork or foam board as outlined above.
- Hold the embroidery over the steam of a kettle for a few minutes.
- Allow to dry and then remove.
- Press with a medium iron on the wrong side.

Here the embroidery has been blocked and mounted, giving it a beautifully taut finish.

MOUNTING YOUR EMBROIDERY

This is a simple but effective way to mount your completed embroidery ready for framing or storing.

MATERIALS REQUIRED

- Acid-free board or foam core
- Felt or thin quilt wadding/batting
- Glue
- Stitchers' tape or acid-free double-sided tape
- Map pins or thumb tacks
- Artists' tape or masking tape

METHOD

- Cut a piece of board to the required size. Cut a piece of felt or wadding/batting the same size. Glue the felt to the top of the board.
- Place your embroidery centrally over the board.
- Insert a few pins along one side to keep it in place.
- Turn over and apply double-sided tape on either side. Pull the fabric up over the tape and secure it in place.
- Repeat on the other side – stretch the fabric, pressing and smoothing it down as you go. Repeat this on the other two sides. Make sure the fabric is taut on the board and there are no creases. Adjust the fabric if necessary.
- Add some artists' or masking tape along the edges of fabric to neaten on the back. Your embroidery is now mounted and ready to frame.

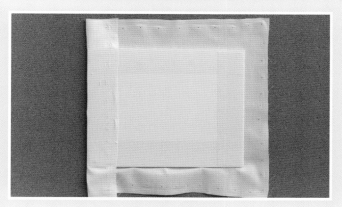

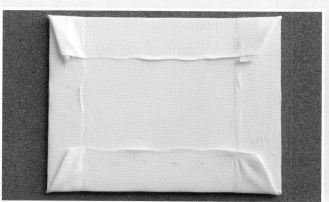

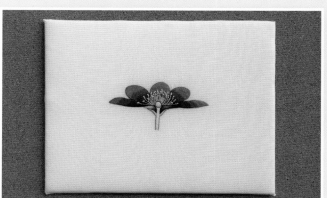

STITCH INSTRUCTIONS

These are the five stitches that best illustrate botanical subjects in needle painting: long-and-short stitch, split stitch, French knots, satin stitch and bullion stitch.

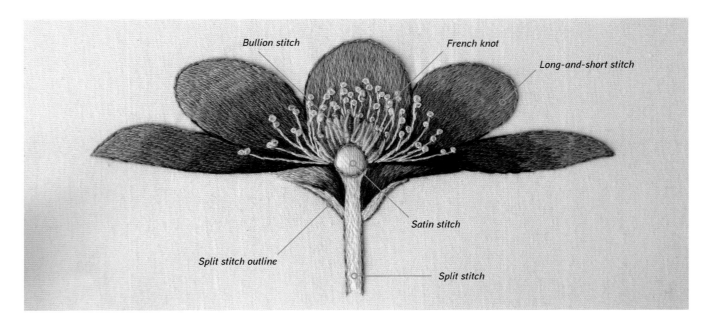

Bullion stitch *French knot* *Long-and-short stitch* *Satin stitch* *Split stitch outline* *Split stitch*

SECURING YOUR THREAD

This method of securing your thread does not leave any lumps or bumps – do not use a knot.

METHOD
- Make a tiny stitch close to the edge of the shape – up at A and down at B. Leave a small tail at the back.
- Make a second stitch close to this – up at C and down at D, into the centre of the first stitch.
- Give it a tug: the thread should be secure. Cut off the tail at the back.
- To finish and start a new colour, run your needle and thread under a few stitches at the back of the work to secure.

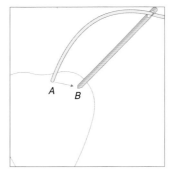 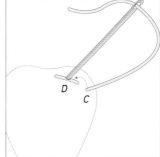

LONG-AND-SHORT STITCH

Long-and-short stitch shading is worked in rows of stitches that softly blend into each other. The colours gradually change through the rows to produce a smooth transition of colour. This colour gradient results in the beautiful shading that long-and-short stitch is so well known for. It can be adapted to fill different shapes and to achieve different effects within individual elements of a design – these are discussed in more depth in the pages that follow.

BASIC LONG-AND-SHORT STITCH FILLING A SIMPLE PETAL

The term long-and-short is confusing, as it is more like staggered satin stitches – so let go of the idea that you need to stitch one long stitch then one short stitch across the row. The stitches in each new row cover the base of the stitches in the previous row.

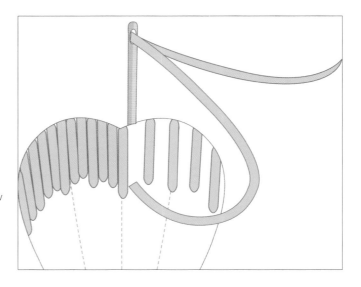

METHOD

Row one: start in the centre of the shape and work out towards each side. Using the lightest shade of colour, add random stitches across the shape to establish the direction of your stitching. Each stitch should be approximately 1cm (½in) in length, up at A and down at B. Continue filling in the gaps with long-and-short stitches across the shape until the row is complete. The stitches in the first row should be very close together to establish a firm foundation for the next rows.

Row two: turn your work around so you are working away from you and looking out onto your stitching. Thread the second shade of colour and again add random stitches across the row as before. Bring the needle up through the previous stitching at A and down into the fabric at B. It works best if you come *up* into the previous stitching and not down. Going down into stitches causes little holes like small pepper marks, which make your stitching look rough and uneven.

Continue filling in the gaps with long-and-short stitch across the shape until the row is complete. Keep your stitches in line with the guidelines, adjusting as necessary to fit the shape. Work every other row as for row two, changing to the next shade of colour each time.

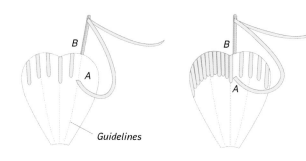

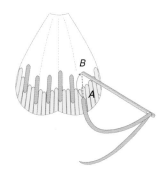

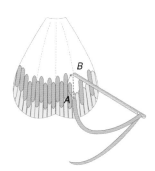

GUIDELINES FOR LONG-AND-SHORT STITCH

Long-and-short stitch shading does not always follow straight lines – sometimes we need to adjust the stitches to follow the direction of a shape and achieve a more natural look. If you look at a petal, for example, you will see that it most often tapers towards the centre. It helps to draw in guidelines to direct your stitches. These can be drawn in with an HB pencil, as shown in the example.

Guidelines

TIPS FOR LONG-AND-SHORT STITCH

Wherever possible, stitch from the wider area to the narrow area of a shape. It is much easier to reduce stitches than it is to increase them. There may be instances where you have no choice due to the nature of the shape, but generally it is easier to stitch from a wide to a narrow area.

Always stagger the stitches in each row to create a soft blending of shades. Avoid rigid bands of stitching. If your rows look straight, go back and add the odd staggered stitch to break up the line.

Always fill each row (particularly the first row) adequately. Avoid leaving gaps in between the stitches, otherwise when you stitch the next row there won't be any thread to go into, just a space. If you see a gap, go back and add in a stitch to fill it.

The stitches in each row should lie parallel to each other. Sometimes you need to gradually change the slant of the stitches to fit a shape but, wherever possible, avoid abrupt changes of angle as this will cause your stitching to look messy.

Do   Avoid

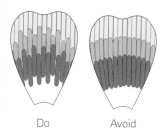

Do   Avoid

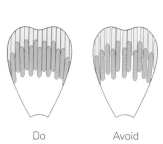

Do   Avoid

Do   Avoid

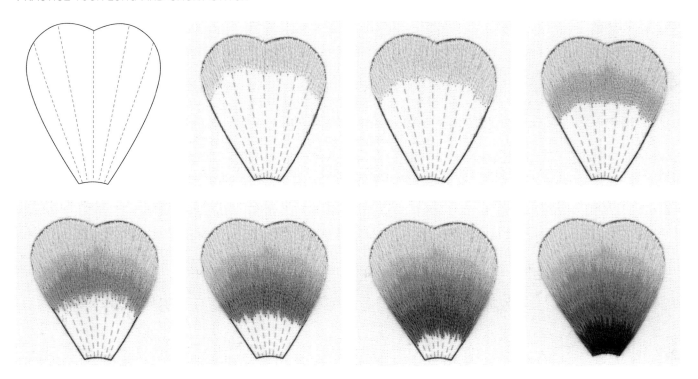

If you are new to embroidery, you may like to familiarize yourself with the basics of long-and-short stitch. Transfer this petal outline with an HB pencil to a scrap of fabric, draw in some guidelines and practise filling it with long-and-short stitch using five shades from light to dark of any colour. Use the step-by-step photographs above as a guide. Don't worry if it does not look right the first time – it will come with a bit of practice!

LONG-AND-SHORT STITCH FOR FLOWERS

Start with the petals that are at the back or bottom and work up to the petals in the front. You can also add a split stitch outline to define each petal (see page 30). Stitch from the outside edge of the petal in towards the centre, as shown in the diagram.

LONG-AND-SHORT STITCH IN A FLOWER WITH 'COMPLEX' PETALS

Here is an example of the stages of stitching long-and-short stitch in a flower with layered and irregular petals. Note how the petals are outlined individually first, then worked from back to front.

 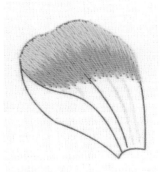 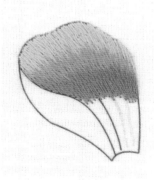

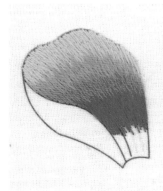  

LONG-AND-SHORT STITCH FOR PETALS WITH A TURNOVER

Stitch the petal first and then the turnover.

- Fill the petal with long-and-short stitch, following the steps on page 21.
- Outline the turnover with split stitch. Pad the turnover with long straight stitches to raise it slightly above the petal (see also pages 32–33).
- On top of this and over the split stitch outline, add long-and-short stitches or satin stitches if space does not allow.

LONG-AND-SHORT STITCH FOR LEAVES

Fill both sides of the leaf, on either side of the centre vein, with long-and-short stitch. Start from the outside edge and work in towards the centre vein. When one side is complete, go back and stitch the other side. The centre vein is stitched with split stitch.

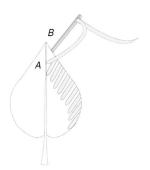 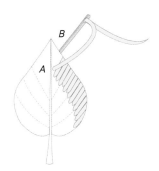 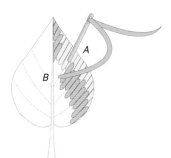 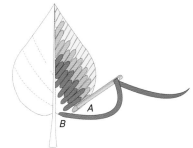

LONG-AND-SHORT STITCH FOR SIMPLE LEAF SHAPES

Draw in guidelines to direct your stitching. Fill each side of the leaf with long-and-short stitch from the outside edge in towards the centre vein, using your guidelines to direct your stitches. Stitch the centre vein with split stitch.

LONG-AND-SHORT STITCH FOR IRREGULAR LEAF SHAPES

To stitch a leaf that has an irregular shape, it is easier to divide each section and stitch individually. You can draw in pencil lines to separate each section, as shown in red in the diagram. Again, start from the outside edge and work in towards the centre vein. Once all the stitching is complete, stitch the centre vein and outlines with split stitch.

LONG-AND-SHORT STITCH FOR SMALL SHAPES

To fill a small shape such as a bud or sepal with more than one shade of colour, do not shorten your stitches to try to fit all the shades into the space. Rather, fill the shape with the two lightest colours, then add a few straight stitches at the base on top of this in the darker shades, as shown in the example, right.

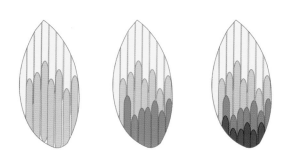

LIGHT AND SHADOW FOR LONG-AND-SHORT STITCH

Light shines on everything, providing highlights in some areas and shadows in others; without light and shadow everything would appear flat and dull. To achieve a realistic three-dimensional appearance in our embroidery we need to include light and shadow. Here is an example where the light source is top-left: everything on the top-left is in light; the bottom-right is in shadow.

Light   *Shadow*

Light   *Shadow*

COLOUR FOR LONG-AND-SHORT STITCH

Contrary to popular belief, long-and-short shading itself is not smooth; as each row encroaches into the previous one it will be slightly raised. It is the smooth transition of colour that makes your shading *appear* smooth. If the shades are correctly blended they will appear to melt into each other and glow. These are the two most important factors:

1. RIGHT BLEND OF SHADES

When shading from light to dark the values should be of similar tones so that they blend easily. You can change contrast, e.g. from pale pink into medium/dark pink and it will look fine, but if you change tones abruptly it will look wrong. To the right you can see an example showing a good blend of blue shades (above) and a less successful blend of blue shades (below). In the first petal you will see that similar tones in the periwinkle blue family create a nice transition of colour, but in the second petal there is a jump from periwinkle blue into Prussian blue tones, which breaks the continuity of shading. This can happen if you substitute one brand of thread for another, or if you use threads from different dye lots, as the colours in different dye lots rarely match.

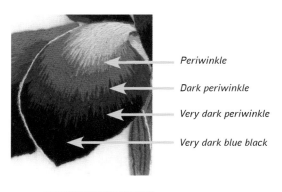

Periwinkle

Dark periwinkle

Very dark periwinkle

Very dark blue black

2. GOOD BALANCE OF SHADES

Achieving the right balance in your shading can contribute enormously to the visual smoothness of the stitching. A simple guide that will help to achieve a good balance is: wherever possible, fill the shape with two-thirds light or medium shades and one-third dark shades, as shown in the examples below.

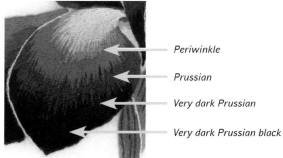

Periwinkle

Prussian

Very dark Prussian

Very dark Prussian black

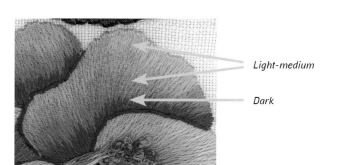

Light-medium

Dark

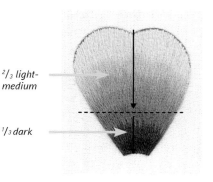

²/₃ light-medium

¹/₃ dark

SPLIT STITCH

Sometimes you might want to use a split stitch outline under your long-and-short stitch to define the edge of a shape. This can be particularly useful when you are stitching a flower with petals that lie one on top of the other. The edge of each petal needs to be raised slightly to define it, otherwise they will look like they all merge into each other.

METHOD

Outline the shape with split stitch. You can use one strand of thread for this but, if the shape is quite large, you can use two strands to make a very raised edge. The long-and-short stitches will go over the split stitch outline, so it will be covered by the long-and-short stitches as shown in the diagram. You can also add a split stitch outline around the completed stitching to define the edges, see page 30.

SPLIT STITCH FILLING

This can be used to fill shapes such as a stem, or when an area is too small for long-and-short stitch, as shown in the example, right.

METHOD

Stitch a line of split stitch. Next to this add another line of split stitch – continue adding adjacent lines of split stitch one next to the other to fill the shape. Please note, you can change the shades of colour (light to dark) either horizontally or vertically in the split stitch lines to create a shaded effect as shown in the examples.

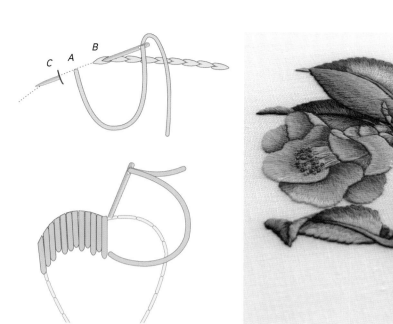

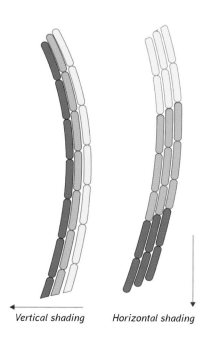

Vertical shading   *Horizontal shading*

FRENCH KNOTS

French knots are used to add texture to an area. They are useful for imitating areas like flower centres, pollen or seeds. French knots can be stitched in different shades of colour to produce a shaded or graduated effect.

METHOD

- Use one strand of thread and two twists. Bring your needle up at A and then wrap the thread around your needle twice.
- Insert your needle tip into the fabric very close to the original hole, at B.
- Pull your thread quite firmly to form a knot against the fabric, then pull the needle through to the back of your fabric to complete the knot.

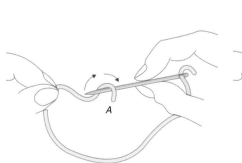
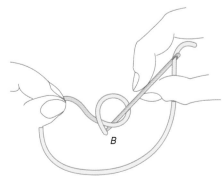
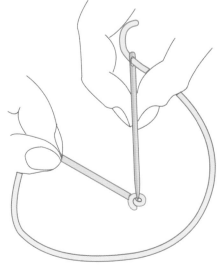

SATIN STITCH

Satin stitch is used to fill shapes with straight parallel stitches. It can be useful if the shape is too small for long-and-short stitch or if the shape to be filled needs a smooth filling.

METHOD

Start slightly away from the edge to establish the direction of your satin stitches; you can go back and fill in the first few stitches afterwards. Come up at A and down at B, as shown in the diagram. Continue to work parallel stitches across the shape.

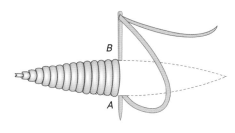

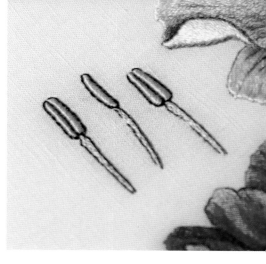

BULLION STITCH

Bullion stitches are used to create coil-like shapes, which can be useful for imitating areas of a flower such as an anther. Note that you will need to slacken the fabric in the hoop or frame to stitch bullions; I often leave them until last so I can do this.

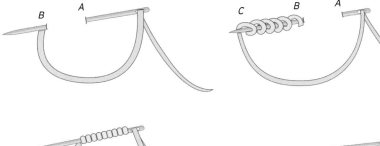

METHOD

- Bring your needle up at B and down at A – this will be the length of your bullion. Only push your needle three-quarters of the way through, leaving a long loop.
- Wind your thread around the needle in an anti-clockwise direction (C). The number of loops will determine the length of the bullion knot.
- Pull your needle gently through the coil of loops and adjust your thread at the same time.
- Pull your needle completely through. Push the top of the coil down while pulling your thread through to even out the coil. Re-insert your needle into the fabric to complete.

PRACTISE THE STITCHES

If you are new to embroidery you may like to familiarize yourself with split stitch, satin stitch, French knots and bullions. Transfer these outlines to a piece of scrap fabric and stitch them using one strand of thread or two if you find it easier to start with. Don't worry if they don't look perfect first time – it will come with a bit of practice.

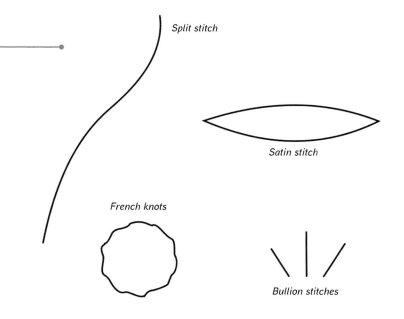

Split stitch

Satin stitch

French knots

Bullion stitches

OUTLINES

Outlines are an effective way of adding details, defining a shape or distinguishing individual aspects of your embroidery. Outlines can make your embroidery pop and add interest to a picture, by making it look more realistic. You can see this in these before and after examples.

Before and after adding outlines.

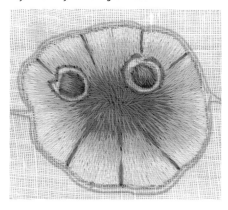 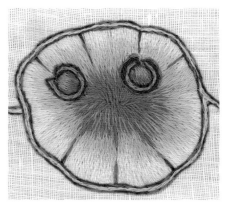 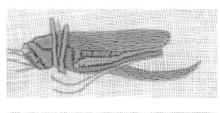 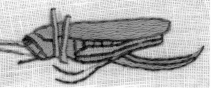

Here I have added outlines and other details to give shape and form to an area of the design. I have embroidered the segments of the bee's wings, and added fine hairs to the sepals of the rosehip.

   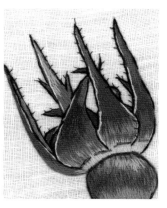

METHOD

The outlines should not dominate your embroidery, rather they should always be fine and subtle. To achieve this, use one strand of thread or, if a very delicate outline is called for, split a strand of polyester sewing thread (see page 13). Rather than stitching a solid line, break up the line occasionally to create a more natural look, as seen in the example, right. Consider choosing dark colours, such as a dark green (right) or dark brown (above), instead of black, which can dominate.

RAISED EMBROIDERY

To create a three-dimensional effect in your embroidery, padding can be added under long-and-short stitch or satin stitch to make shapes look as though they are raised above the fabric. The raised shape creates its own little shadows, which makes it look more lifelike. This is especially effective when used for shapes such as flower buds, sepals, seeds and petal turnovers.

PADDED LONG-AND-SHORT STITCH

Shapes can first be padded with long, straight stitches and then long-and-short stitch worked on top of the padding. It is not recommended that you add more than one or two layers of padding for long-and-short stitch as, if it is too thick, it will be very difficult to get the needle through.

METHOD

- Outline your shape with split stitch so that it will hug the padding and define the edge.
- Fill your shape with straight stitches across the shape – this is the padding, which is always worked at right angles to the long-and-short stitches – as shown in the diagram.
- Stitch long-and-short stitch on top of this and over the split stitch outline.

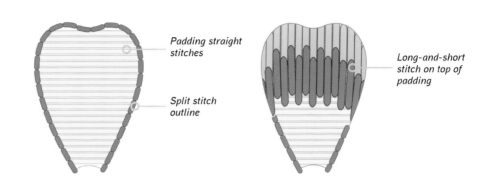

Padding straight stitches

Split stitch outline

Long-and-short stitch on top of padding

Here are two examples of padded long-and-short stitch on a bud and rosebud sepals.

PADDED SATIN STITCH

METHOD

- Outline the shape with split stitch, so that it will hug the padding and define the edge.
- Fill the shape with straight stitches across the shape – this padding should always be worked at right angles to the satin stitch. You can add one, two or three layers of padding for satin stitch.
- Stitch the satin stitch on top of this and over the split stitch outline.

Padding straight stitches   *Outline split stitch*

Satin stitches on top of padding

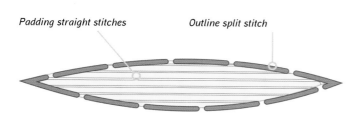
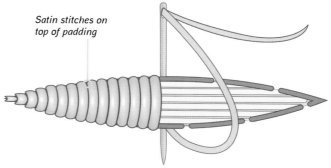

Here is an example of padded satin stitch on a blackberry. Each portion of the blackberry is stitched in padded satin stitch to make it stand out.

ANATOMY OF A FLOWER

The parts of a flower and the structure of a flower are illustrated here to help you easily identify the terms used for each project.

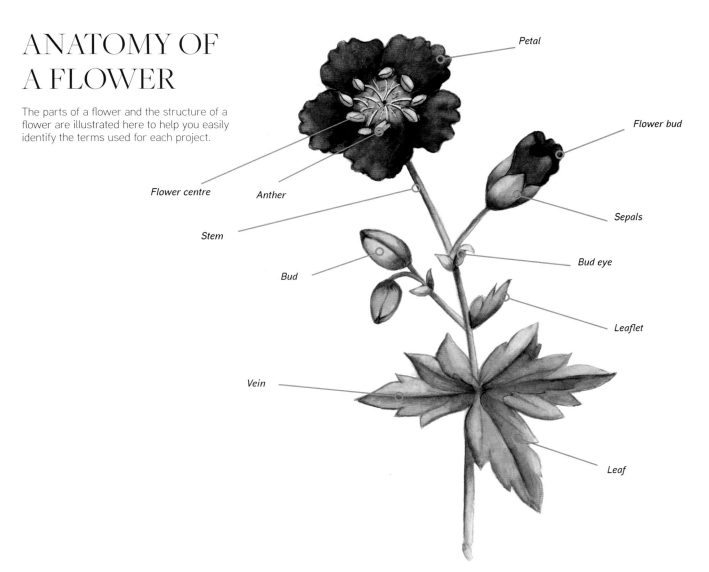

Petal

Flower bud

Flower centre

Anther

Sepals

Stem

Bud

Bud eye

Leaflet

Vein

Leaf

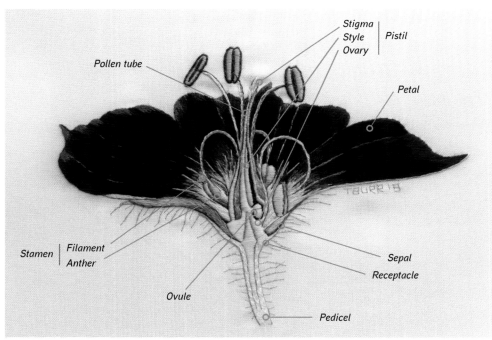

Stigma
Style
Ovary

Pistil

Pollen tube

Petal

Stamen | Filament
Anther

Sepal

Receptacle

Ovule

Pedicel

The flowers of different plants may look different, but all contain the same anatomical elements.

USEFUL ADVICE BEFORE YOU START

- Keep your hands clean.
- To keep your embroidery clean, store it in a white cotton bag or pillowcase.
- Always keep your fabric taut in the hoop or frame.
- Ensure that you are sitting comfortably and take regular breaks. To prevent neck and shoulder tension, try placing a small cushion under your armpit (the side that holds the hoop). This encourages your arm and shoulder into a more relaxed position.
- Stop stitching occasionally and hold your work away from you so you can view it from afar – this gives a truer impression of what it looks like, rather than close up under the magnifying glass.
- If your embroidery doesn't look right, take a photograph of it with your smartphone; if something is wrong, you will immediately see it in the photograph and can then correct it. The wonderful thing about needle painting is that you can often add stitches on top of the previous embroidery or make corrections without unpicking... I really hate unpicking!
- Put on some good music, a podcast, audio book or movie, and enjoy your stitching time.

SIMPLE
PROJECTS

STARTER PROJECT

JAPANESE ANEMONE
ANEMONE JAPONICA

Hand drawn by Trish Burr.

Actual size

PROJECT SIZE

7.5 x 8.5cm (3 x 3½in)

YOU WILL NEED

- Piece of fabric, 28 x 28cm (11 x 11in)
- Threads as per list, opposite
- A super grip hoop or stretcher frame, size 15.25cm (6in)

ORDER OF WORK

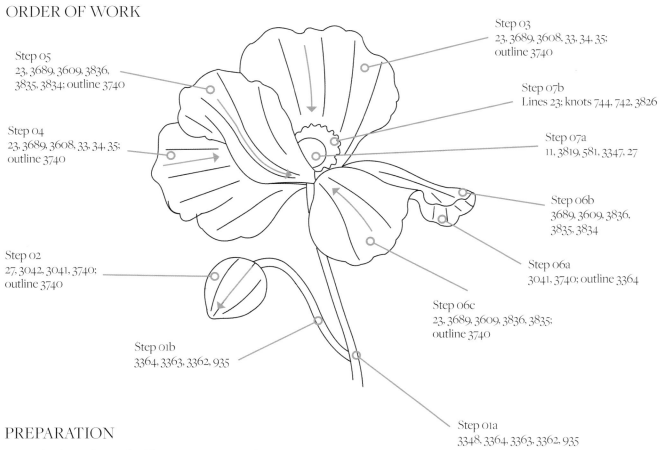

Step 05
23, 3689, 3609, 3836, 3835, 3834; outline 3740

Step 04
23, 3689, 3608, 33, 34, 35; outline 3740

Step 02
27, 3042, 3041, 3740; outline 3740

Step 01b
3364, 3363, 3362, 935

Step 03
23, 3689, 3608, 33, 34, 35; outline 3740

Step 07b
Lines 23; knots 744, 742, 3826

Step 07a
11, 3819, 581, 3347, 27

Step 06b
3689, 3609, 3836, 3835, 3834

Step 06a
3041, 3740; outline 3364

Step 06c
23, 3689, 3609, 3836, 3835; outline 3740

Step 01a
3348, 3364, 3363, 3362, 935

PREPARATION

- Transfer the outline to the fabric (see pages 16 and 164).
- Mount your fabric in the hoop (see page 17).
- Follow the step-by-step instructions on pages 40–43.

THREAD LIST

DMC
- 11
- 23
- 27
- 33
- 34
- 35
- 581
- 742
- 744
- 935
- 3041
- 3042
- 3347
- 3348
- 3362
- 3363
- 3364
- 3608
- 3609
- 3689
- 3740
- 3819
- 3826
- 3834
- 3835
- 3836

STEP 01: STEMS
Fill the stems with adjacent rows of split stitch.

STEP 02: BUD
Fill the bud with long-and-short stitch. Outline with split stitch.

STEP 03: PETAL
Fill the petal with long-and-short stitch.

STEP 04: PETAL
Fill the petal with long-and-short stitch.

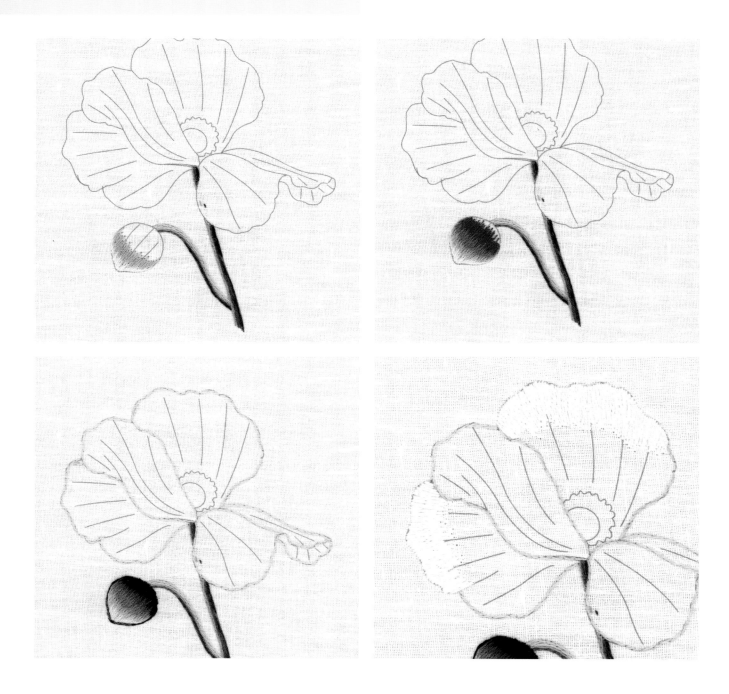

STEP 03: PETAL

Fill the petal with long-and-short stitch.

STEP 04: PETAL

Fill the petal with long-and-short stitch.

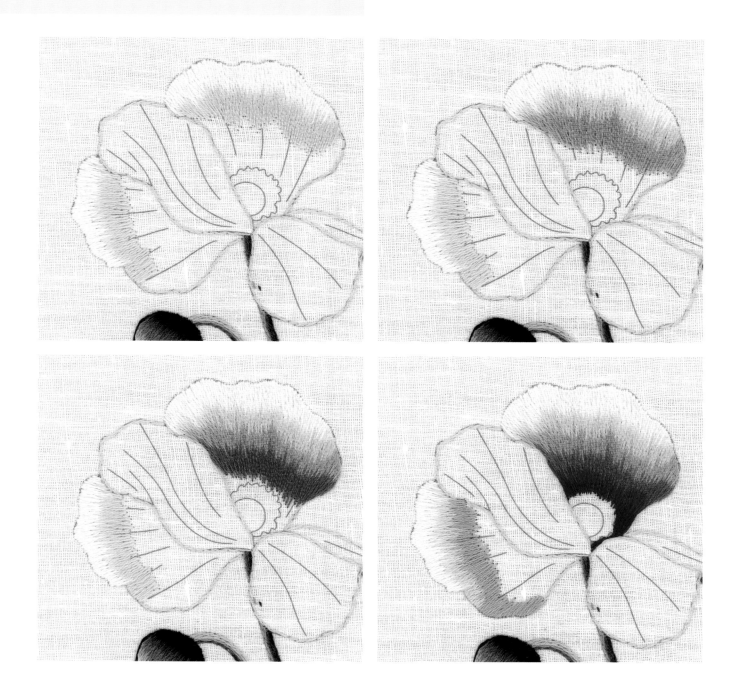

STEP 03: PETAL
Fill the petal with long-and-short stitch. Outline with split stitch.

STEP 04: PETAL
Fill the petal with long-and-short stitch. Outline with split stitch.

STEP 05: PETAL
Fill the petal with long-and-short stitch. Outline with split stitch.

STEP 06: PETAL
Fill each part of the petal, including the underside, with long-and-short stitch. Outline with split stitch.

STEP 07: FLOWER CENTRE

7a. Fill the centre with French knots; use one strand and two twists.

7b. Add straight lines around the centre. Add French knots on top of this, using one strand and two twists. Use the photographs, right, as a guide.

FLOWER SAMPLER

Based on a painting called the Magenta Flower Line by Rachel Pedder-Smith, this sampler project includes eighteen small elements that can be stitched together or individually. The instructions for each element are listed separately over the following pages.

To stitch the full sampler, use a hoop and keep the relevant area of fabric in view while stitching. Roll up the fabric that is not in use and make a few tacking/basting stitches to keep it out of the way. Once you have completed the first elements, remove your hoop and mount it for the next two elements, again rolling up the fabric as needed. Continue in this manner until the sampler is complete. You will need to block it on a large board to remove the creases when finished (see page 18).

PROJECT SIZE
12 x 68cm (4¾ x 26¾in)

YOU WILL NEED
- Piece of fabric, 35 x 90cm (13¾ x 35½in)
- Threads as per list for each element
- A super grip hoop, size 20cm (8 in)

PREPARATION
- Transfer the outline to the fabric (see pages 16 and 164–167).
- Mount the fabric in the hoop (see page 17).
- Follow the step-by-step instructions on pages 46–93.
- Move the hoop across the fabric while stitching and roll the excess fabric up. You can put a tacking/basting stitch in to hold the fabric in place while you are stitching.

1 2 3 4 5 6 7 8

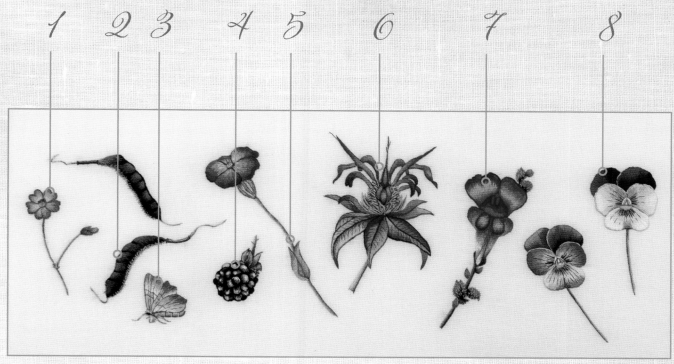

9 10 11 12 13 14 15 16 17 18

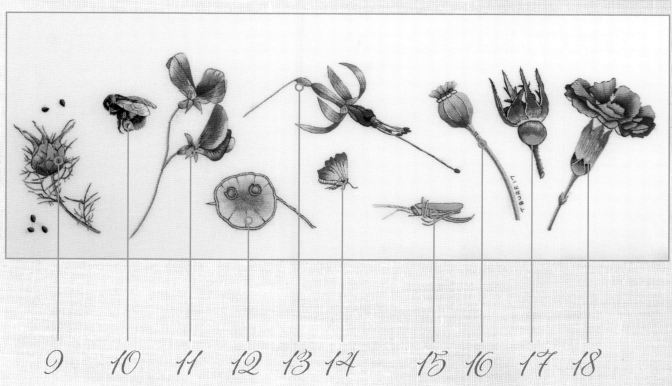

THREAD LIST

DMC	
- 209	- 3012
- 372	- 3013
- 520	- 3363
- 554	- 3609
- 3011	- 3787
	- 3835

ORDER OF WORK

Actual size

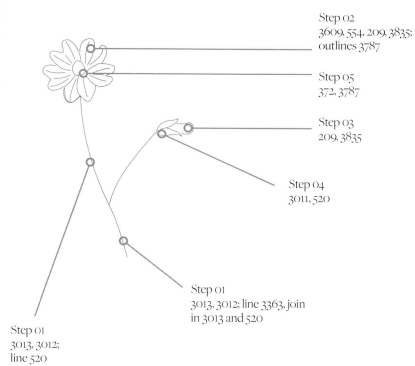

Step 02
3609, 554, 209, 3835;
outlines 3787

Step 05
372, 3787

Step 03
209, 3835

Step 04
3011, 520

Step 01
3013, 3012; line 3363, join
in 3013 and 520

Step 01
3013, 3012;
line 520

STEP 01: STEMS
Fill with adjacent rows of split stitch.

STEP 02: FLOWER PETALS
Fill with long-and-short stitch, then outline with split stitch.

STEP 03: BUD
Fill with long-and-short stitch.

STEP 04: SEPALS
Fill with long-and-short stitch.

STEP 05: FLOWER CENTRE
Fill with French knots; make all outlines in split stitch.

2 PEA PODS

THREAD LIST

DMC
- 610
- 844
- 3011
- 3013
- 3371
- 3781
- Hairs:
  646 or
  polycotton

ORDER OF WORK

Actual size

Step 01
610, 3781, 844, 3371; outline 3371

STEP 01: PODS
Outline the pods with split stitch. Fill each section with long-and-short stitch. Add darker shades between.

STEP 02: STEM
Fill with split stitches, then outline with split stitch.

STEP 03: TENDRIL
Fill with split stitch.

STEP 04: POD HAIRS
Add tiny criss-crossing hairs along one side of each pod with one strand of 646 or match a polycotton sewing thread in a similar shade and split it in half for a very fine thread.

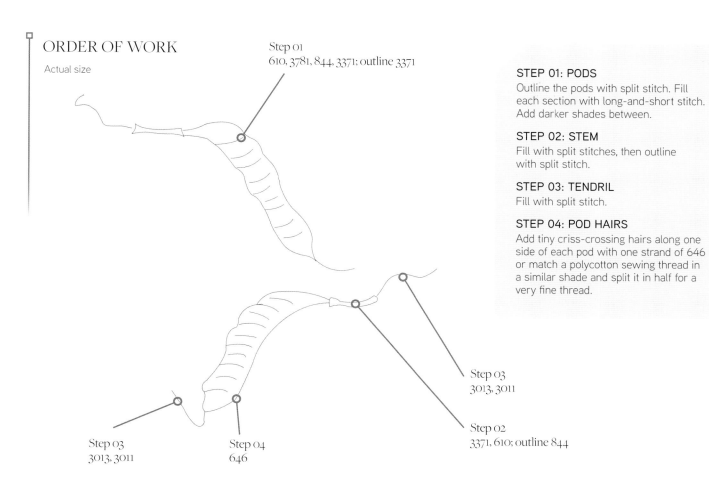

Step 03
3013, 3011

Step 02
3371, 610; outline 844

Step 03
3013, 3011

Step 04
646

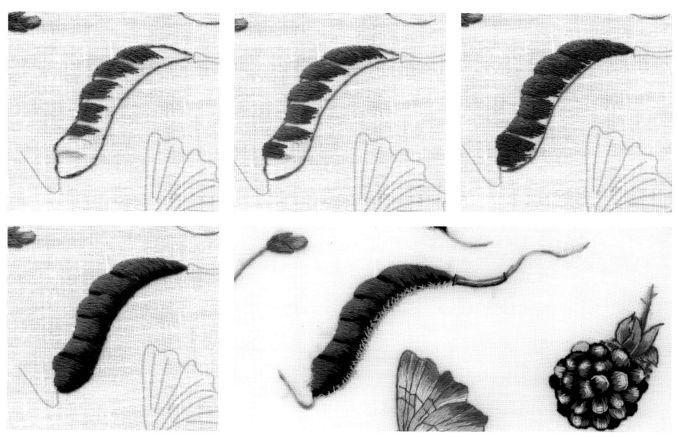

THREAD LIST

DMC	
- 435	- 3371
- 436	- 3823
- 437	- 3826
- 646	- 3855
- 738	- Lines:
- 975	434 or
	polycotton

ORDER OF WORK

Actual size

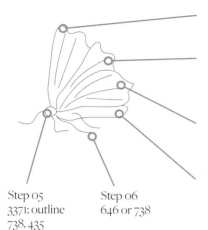

Step 02
3826, 435, 437, 3823, 738; outlines 434

Step 03
975, 3826, 437, 738

Step 04
975, 3826, 437, 738, 3823

Step 01
436; stripes 3855, 975; outlines 434

Step 05
3371; outline
738, 435

Step 06
646 or 738

STEP 01: BODY
Fill each segment with padded satin stitch. Add straight stitches for the stripes.

STEP 02: BACK WING
Fill with long-and-short stitch.

STEP 03: MID-WING
Fill with long-and-short stitch.

STEP 04: FRONT WING
Fill with long-and-short stitch.

STEP 05: HEAD AND EYE
Make a French knot for the eye with two twists. Add straight stitches in 738 and 435 around this.

STEP 06: FEELERS
Fill with split stitch.

LINES, OUTLINES AND VEINS
Add straight lines in one strand of 434 or match up a similar shade in polycotton and split the strand in half for a fine thread.

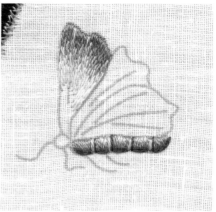

BLACKBERRY
RUBUS FRUTICOSUS

4

THREAD LIST

DMC
- 310
- 317
- 372
- 415
- 520
- Blanc
- 522
- 611
- 3011
- 3013
- 3021
- 3781

ORDER OF WORK

Actual size

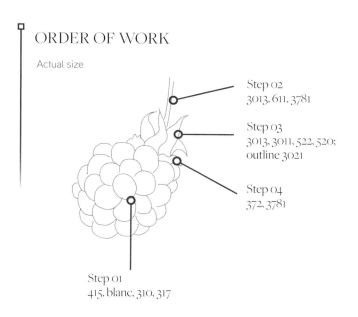

Step 02
3013, 611, 3781

Step 03
3013, 3011, 522, 520;
outline 3021

Step 04
372, 3781

Step 01
415, blanc, 310, 317

STEP 01: BLACKBERRY

Add outlines in 310. Pad each ball with one strand of 415. Fill on top of this with satin stitch in 317. Add a highlight in 415 and blanc (place tiny stitches in each). Add shadows in 310.

Padding 415   Satin Stitch 317

Highlight 415 and blanc
Shadow 310

STEP 02: STEM

Fill the stem with split stitch. Add two thorns in straight stitches.

STEP 03: SEPALS

Fill the sepals with long-and-short stitch. Outline in split stitch.

STEP 04: FRENCH KNOTS

Add French knots underneath the leaves in 372 and 3781; use one strand and two twists for each.

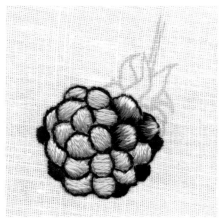

THREAD LIST
DMC
Prefaced with a 'D'
in the steps.
- 150
- 320
- 3013
- 3021
- 3052
- 3053
- 3350
- 3363
- 3687
- 3688
- 3787

Anchor
Prefaced with
an 'A' in the steps.
- 66
- 73
- 74

ORDER OF WORK

Actual size

Step 04a
A66, D3350

Step 04b
D150, D3350, D3688, A73, A74

Step 04e
D150, D3350, D3687, D3688, A74

Step 05
D3013; outline
D3021

Step 04c
D150, D3350,
D3688, A73, A74

Step 03
D3013, D3053, D3052, D320;
outline D3787

Step 04d
D150, D3350,
D3687, D3688, A74

Step 02
D3013, D3053, D3052,
D3363, D320; outline D3787

Step 01
D3013, D3053, D3052,
D3363, D320; outline D3787

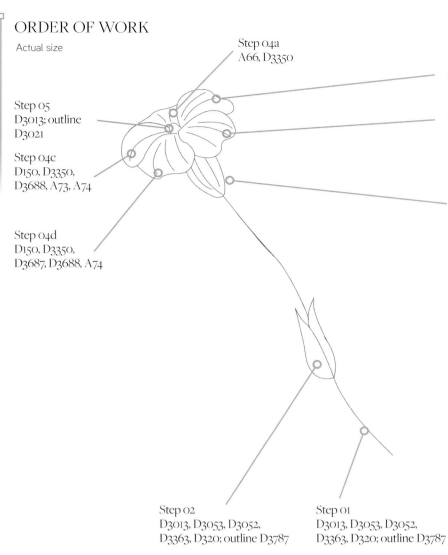

STEP 01: STEM
Fill with adjacent rows of split stitch. Add a line of split stitch along the right-hand side in a dark shade.

STEP 02: SEPALS
Fill with adjacent rows of split stitch. Outline with split stitch.

STEP 03: RECEPTACLE
Fill each section with long-and-short stitch. Outline with split stitch.

STEP 04: PETALS
Fill each petal with long-and-short stitch from the outside edge in towards the centre. Outline with split stitch.

STEP 05: FLOWER CENTRE
Fill with straight stitches. Add a tiny French knot on the tip.

LOVE-IN-A-MIST SEED HEAD
NIGELLA DAMASCENA

THREAD
LIST

DMC
- 150
- 152
- 154
- 223
- 310
- 315
- 352
- 402
- 415
- 754
- 778
- 801
- 844
- 902
- 945
- 3021
- 3023
- 3350
- 3371
- 3687
- 3688
- 3712
- 3778
- 3803
- 3857

ORDER OF WORK
Actual size

Step 04
3712, 3687, 3350, 150, 902; outline 3371

Step 03b
3712, 3687, 3350, 150;
outline 3371

Step 03a
3712, 3687, 3803, 3857;
outline 3371

Step 05
310, 844, 3023, 415; lines 3021

Step 06
778, 3688, 844

Step 02f
754, 152, 223, 3687, 3803

Step 02g
402, 3712, 3687, 3688,
3803, 902

Step 02e
754, 152, 223, 3687, 3803

Step 02b
3712, 3687, 3803

**Centre veins and
outlines 154 and
902; fine veins use
polycotton similar
to 3021 or 3371**

Step 02a
402, 3778, 223, 315;
add 3687, 315

Step 02d
3712, 3687, 3803, 902

Step 02c
402, 352, 3712, 3687, 315

Step 01
945, 402, 3778; outline 801

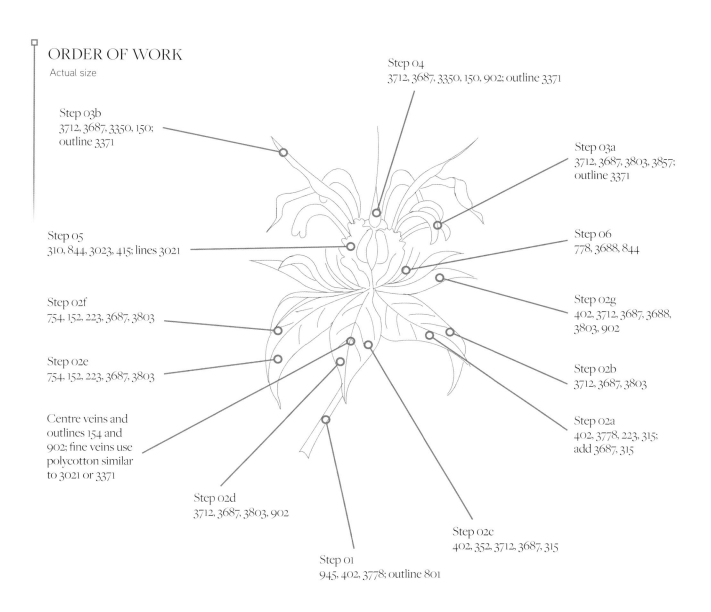

STEP 01: STEM
Fill the stem with adjacent rows of split stitch.

Above: and right: completing lower petals 2a–2g.

STEP 02: LOWER PETALS

Fill each petal (a–g) with long-and-short stitch. Work on either side of the centre vein from the outside in towards the centre. Add the centre vein in split stitch. Add the outline and fine veins in split stitch.

STEP 03: UPPER PETALS

Fill the upper petals with long-and-short stitch. Outline in split stitch.

STEP 04: FLOWER CENTRE

Fill each section with long-and-short stitch, or satin stitch where space does not allow. Outline the sections in split stitch. Use the enlarged photograph on page 56 for colour placement and detail.

Above: completing the upper petals.
Right: completing the upper petals and the flower centre.

STEP 05: AROUND CENTRE

Add straight lines in different shades. Refer to the photographs top left, top right and above for details.

STEP 06: BELOW CENTRE

Fill each line with split stitch – refer to the photograph, right, for details.

7 SNAPDRAGON
ANTIRRHINUM MAJUS

THREAD LIST

DMC
Prefaced with a 'D' in the steps.
- 150
- 451
- 452
- 522
- 601
- 602
- 603
- 611
- 779
- 938
- 962
- 963
- 3021
- 3371
- 3685
- 3687
- 3726
- 3803
- 3860

Anchor
Prefaced with an 'A' in the steps.
- 27
- 28
- 29
- 59

ORDER OF WORK

Actual size

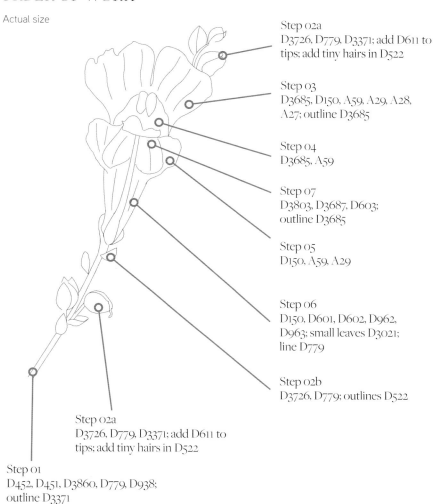

Step 02a
D3726, D779, D3371; add D611 to
tips; add tiny hairs in D522

Step 03
D3685, D150, A59, A29, A28,
A27; outline D3685

Step 04
D3685, A59

Step 07
D3803, D3687, D603;
outline D3685

Step 05
D150, A59, A29

Step 06
D150, D601, D602, D962,
D963; small leaves D3021;
line D779

Step 02b
D3726, D779; outlines D522

Step 02a
D3726, D779, D3371; add D611 to
tips; add tiny hairs in D522

Step 01
D452, D451, D3860, D779, D938;
outline D3371

STEP 01: STEM
Fill with adjacent rows of split stitch.
Add a line on the right side in D3371.

STEP 02: SMALL LEAVES
Add padding stitches to the leaves then
fill with long-and-short stitch. Add tiny
hairs in small straight stitches.

STEP 03: TOP PETALS
Fill the petals with long-and-short stitch.
Outline in split stitch.

STEP 04: CENTRE
Fill with long-and-short stitch. Outline shapes with split stitch.

STEP 05: LOWER PETALS
Fill with long-and-short stitch. Outline with split stitch.

STEP 06: BASE OF PETALS
Fill with long-and-short stitch. Outline with split stitch.

STEP 07: PETAL MARKINGS
Fill with long-and-short stitch. Outline with split stitch.

8 PANSIES
VIOLA TRICOLOR

THREAD LIST

DMC
Prefaced with a
'D' in the steps.
- 154
- 223
- 316
- 437
- 762
- 935
- 3013
- 3051
- 3052
- 3823
- 3834
- 3835
- 3836
- 3854
- 3865
- Blanc

Anchor
Prefaced with an
'A' in the steps.
- 301
- 302
- 342
- 870
- 970
- 972

ORDER OF WORK
Actual size

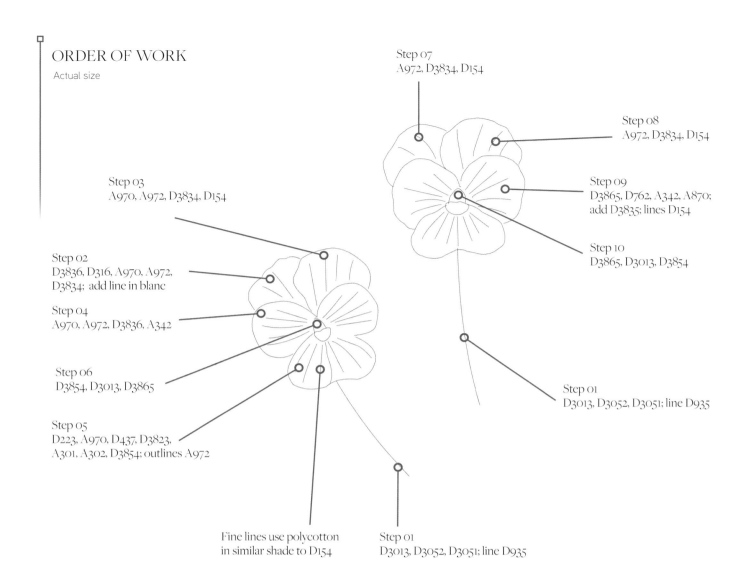

Step 07
A972, D3834, D154

Step 08
A972, D3834, D154

Step 09
D3865, D762, A342, A870;
add D3835; lines D154

Step 10
D3865, D3013, D3854

Step 03
A970, A972, D3834, D154

Step 02
D3836, D316, A970, A972,
D3834; add line in blanc

Step 04
A970, A972, D3836, A342

Step 06
D3854, D3013, D3865

Step 05
D223, A970, D437, D3823,
A301, A302, D3854; outlines A972

Step 01
D3013, D3052, D3051; line D935

Fine lines use polycotton
in similar shade to D154

Step 01
D3013, D3052, D3051; line D935

STEP 01: STEMS
Fill with adjacent rows of split stitch.

STEP 02: BACK PETAL
Fill with long-and-short stitch.
Add outlines in split stitch.

STEP 03: MIDDLE PETAL
Fill with long-and-short stitch.
Add outlines in split stitch.

STEP 04: SIDE PETALS
Fill with long-and-short stitch.
Add outlines in split stitch.

STEP 05: FRONT PETAL
Fill with long-and-short stitch.
Add outlines in split stitch.

STEP 06: FLOWER CENTRE
Fill centre shapes with satin stitch.
Add lines in split stitch.

THREAD LIST

DMC
Prefaced with a 'D'
in the steps.
- 451
- 452
- 3371
- 3782
- 3787

Anchor
Prefaced with an 'A'
in the steps.
- 903
- 904
- 1017

ORDER OF WORK

Actual size

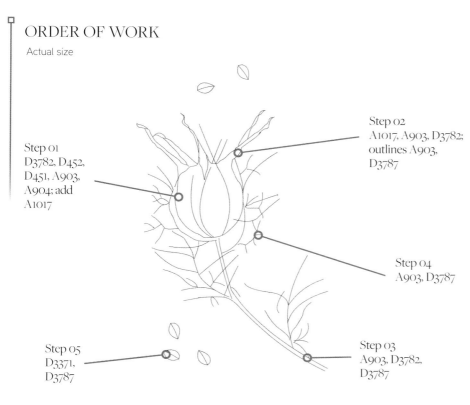

Step 01
D3782, D452,
D451, A903,
A904; add
A1017

Step 02
A1017, A903, D3782;
outlines A903,
D3787

Step 04
A903, D3787

Step 05
D3371,
D3787

Step 03
A903, D3782,
D3787

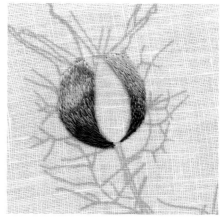

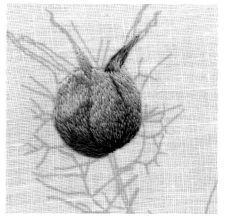

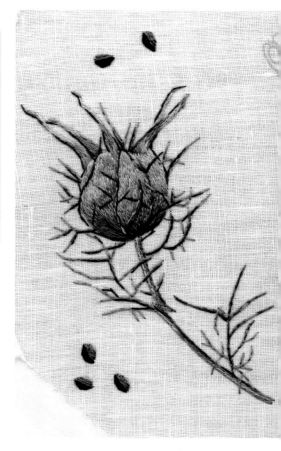

STEP 01: POD
Fill each section of the pod with long-and-short stitch; add lines in split stitch.

STEP 02: SEPALS
Fill the sepals with long-and-short stitch; outline with split stitch.

STEP 03: STEM
Fill the stem with adjacent rows of split stitch.

STEP 04: SPIKY LEAVES
Add spiky lines outside the pod with split stitch – refer to the photograph, right.

STEP 05: SEEDS
Fill the seeds with satin stitch.

THREAD LIST
DMC
- 301
- 310
- 317
- 318
- 437
- 612
- 613
- 645
- 742
- 801
- 976
- 3021
- 3371
- 3782
- 3865
- 3866

ORDER OF WORK

Actual size

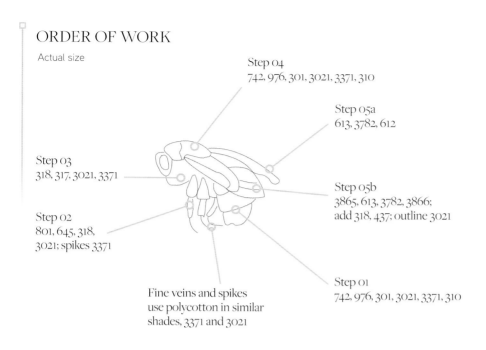

Step 04
742, 976, 301, 3021, 3371, 310

Step 05a
613, 3782, 612

Step 03
318, 317, 3021, 3371

Step 05b
3865, 613, 3782, 3866;
add 318, 437; outline 3021

Step 02
801, 645, 318,
3021; spikes 3371

Fine veins and spikes
use polycotton in similar
shades, 3371 and 3021

Step 01
742, 976, 301, 3021, 3371, 310

STEP 01: ABDOMEN
Fill the sections with irregular long-and-short stitch. Work in layers, one on top of the other.

STEP 02: LEGS
Fill the legs with adjacent rows of split stitch. Outline with split stitch. Add tiny stitches for the spikes.

STEP 03: EYE AND FEELERS
Fill the eye and feelers with satin stitch. Outline with split stitch. Fill the area around this with irregular long-and-short stitches.

STEP 04: UPPER THORAX
Fill with irregular long-and-short stitches.

STEP 05: WINGS
Fill wings with long-and-short stitch. Outline with split stitch. Add fine veins on top of this in split stitches or straight stitch. For the front wing (5b), fill wings with long-and-short stitch in 3865, 613, 3782, 3866. On top of this add long-and-short stitches in 318 and 437 to make it look slightly transparent. Add veins in 3021.

SWEET PEA
LATHYRUS ODORATUS

THREAD LIST

DMC
Prefaced with a 'D'
in the steps.
- 153
- 154
- 371
- 372
- 553
- 829
- 3021
- 3348
- 3350
- 3363
- 3364
- 3835
- 3836
- Veins and
  outlines: 154
  and 3021 or
  polycotton

Anchor
Prefaced with an
'A' in the steps.
- 39
- 73
- 74
- 75
- 108
- 109
- 110
- 119
- 401
- 972

ORDER OF WORK

Actual size

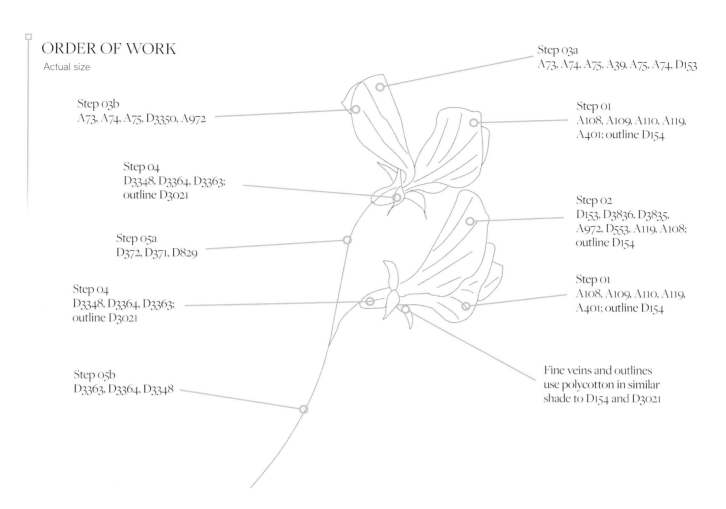

Step 03a
A73, A74, A75, A39, A75, A74, D153

Step 03b
A73, A74, A75, D3350, A972

Step 01
A108, A109, A110, A119, A401; outline D154

Step 04
D3348, D3364, D3363; outline D3021

Step 02
D153, D3836, D3835, A972, D553, A119, A108; outline D154

Step 05a
D372, D371, D829

Step 04
D3348, D3364, D3363; outline D3021

Step 01
A108, A109, A110, A119, A401; outline D154

Step 05b
D3363, D3364, D3348

Fine veins and outlines use polycotton in similar shade to D154 and D3021

STEP 01: PETALS

Fill with long-and-short stitch from the outside edge in towards the centre. Outline the petals with split stitch.

STEP 02: PETAL
Fill with long-and-short stitch from the outside edge in towards the centre. Add an outline with split stitch.

STEP 03: PETAL
Fill with long-and-short stitch from the outside edge in towards the centre. Add an outline with split stitch.

STEP 04: SEPALS
Fill with long-and-short stitch. Outline in split stitch.

STEP 05: STEMS
Fill with adjacent rows of split stitch. Add all outlines and veins in split stitch – refer to the photograph opposite.

THREAD LIST

DMC
- 435
- 436
- 437
- 611
- 612
- 738
- 739
- 3781

ORDER OR WORK

Actual size

Step 02
612, 611; edge 612; outline 3781

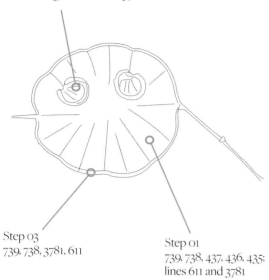

Step 03
739, 738, 3781, 611

Step 01
739, 738, 437, 436, 435;
lines 611 and 3781

STEP 01: SEED CASE
Fill with long-and-short stitch. Work from the
outside edge in towards the centre.

STEP 02: SEEDS
Outline the outer and inner edges with split stitch.
Fill with satin stitch.

STEP 03: OUTSIDE EDGE
Fill with adjacent rows of split stitch.

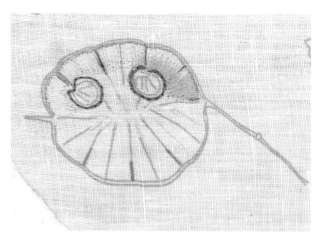

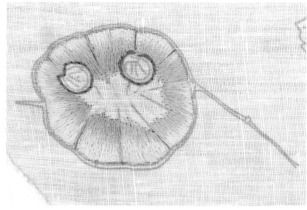

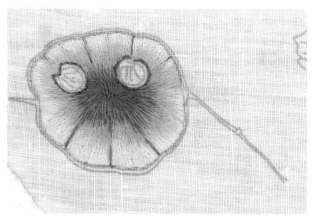

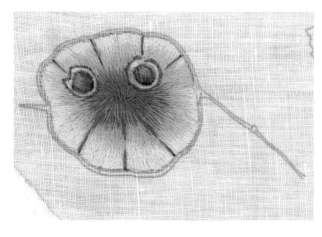

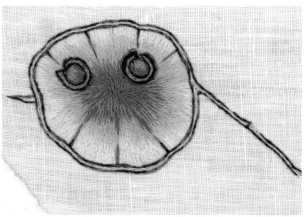

13 FUCHSIA
FUCHSIA MAGELLANICA

THREAD LIST

DMC
Prefaced with a 'D' in the steps.
- 154
- 327
- 335
- 370
- 402
- 834
- 3011
- 3350
- 3371
- 3687
- 3746
- 3777
- 3787
- 3803
- 3834
- 3857
- Veins and outlines: 3777 and 3857 or polycotton

Anchor
Prefaced with an 'A' in the steps.
- 8
- 9
- 10
- 11
- 13

ORDER OF WORK

Actual size

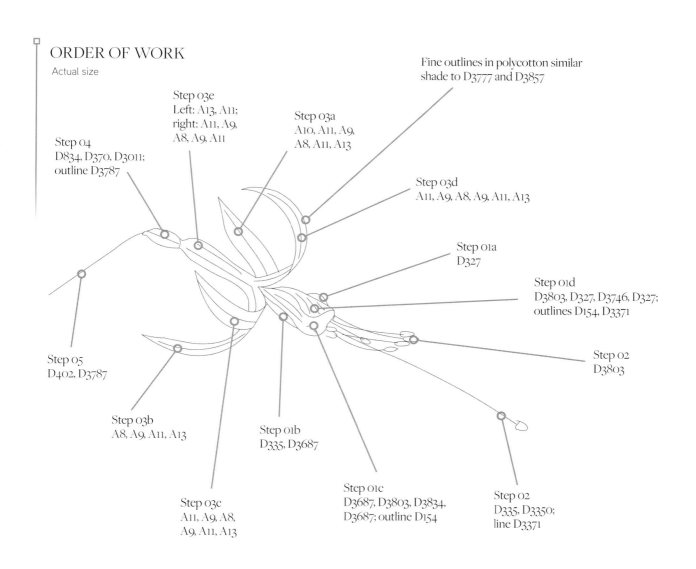

Step 03e
Left: A13, A11;
right: A11, A9,
A8, A9, A11

Step 03a
A10, A11, A9,
A8, A11, A13

Fine outlines in polycotton similar
shade to D3777 and D3857

Step 04
D834, D370, D3011;
outline D3787

Step 03d
A11, A9, A8, A9, A11, A13

Step 01a
D327

Step 01d
D3803, D327, D3746, D327;
outlines D154, D3371

Step 05
D402, D3787

Step 02
D3803

Step 03b
A8, A9, A11, A13

Step 01b
D335, D3687

Step 03c
A11, A9, A8,
A9, A11, A13

Step 01c
D3687, D3803, D3834,
D3687; outline D154

Step 02
D335, D3350;
line D3371

STEP 01: INNER PETALS
Fill each section with long-and-short
stitch. Outline with split stitch.

STEP 02: STAMENS AND PISTIL

Fill each stamen with adjacent rows of split stitch. Fill the anthers with satin stitch.

STEP 03: OUTER PETALS AND TUBE

Fill each petal with long-and-short stitch. Add fine outlines and veins in split stitch. Fill the tube in two parts: left and right.

STEP 04: OVARY

Fill the ovary with long-and-short stitch. Outline with split stitch.

STEP 05: STEM

Fill the stem with adjacent rows of split stitch – refer to the photograph on page 78.

THREAD LIST
DMC
- 611
- 712
- 834
- 844
- 3021
- 3047
- 3787

ORDER OF WORK

Actual size

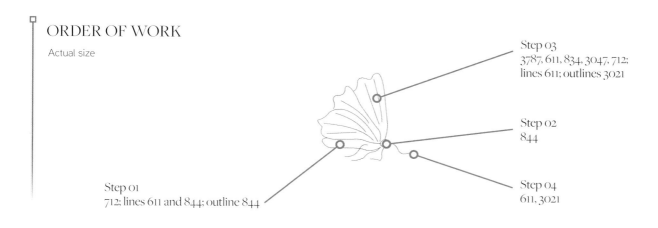

Step 03
3787, 611, 834, 3047, 712;
lines 611; outlines 3021

Step 02
844

Step 04
611, 3021

Step 01
712; lines 611 and 844; outline 844

STEP 01: BODY
Fill with padded satin stitch. Add straight lines across the shape.

STEP 02: HEAD
Fill the head with padded satin stitch. Outline with split stitch.

STEP 03: WINGS
Fill the wings with long-and-short stitch from the outside edge in towards the centre. Outline with split stitch.

STEP 04: LEGS AND FEELERS
Fill feelers and legs with split stitch.

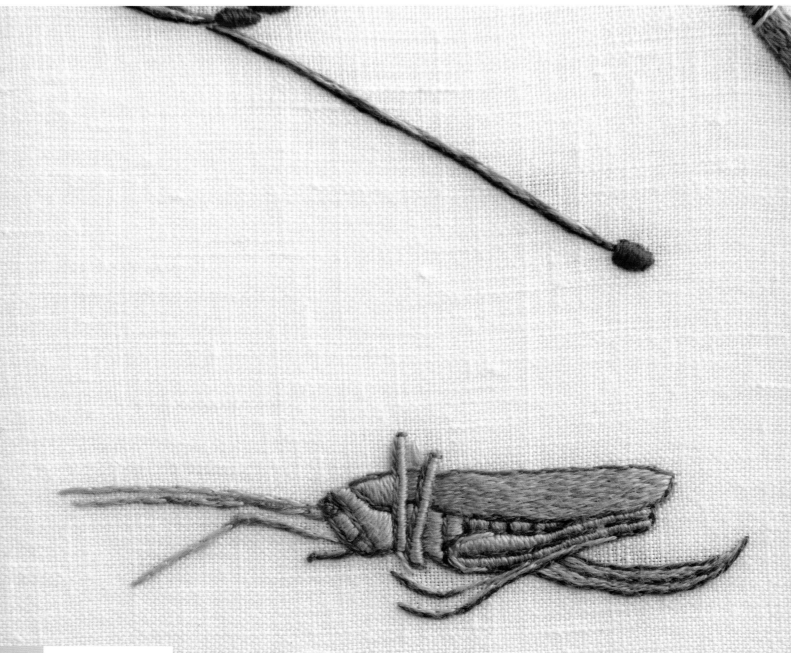

THREAD LIST
DMC
- 368
- 524
- 611
- 3013
- 3046
- 3787

ORDER OF WORK
Actual size

Step 04
3046, 3013

Step 03
368, 524, 3013

Outlines 611, 3787

Step 01
3013, 524

Step 01
3013, 524

Step 05
3046, 611, 3787

Step 02
524

Step 04
3046, 3013

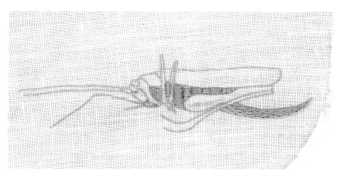

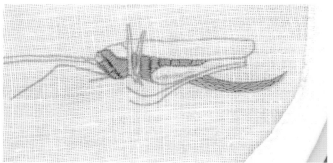

STEP 01: THORAX AND ABDOMEN
Fill the thorax with satin stitch. Fill the abdomen with adjacent rows of split stitch. Add straight lines between; outline with split stitch.

STEP 02: HEAD
Fill sections with satin stitch, then outline with split stitch. Make a French knot for the eye.

STEP 03: WINGS
Fill with long-and-short stitch. Outline with split stitch.

STEP 04: FRONT AND BACK LEGS
Fill legs with tiny satin stitches; outline with split stitch.

STEP 05: ANTENNAE
Fill with adjacent rows of split stitch.

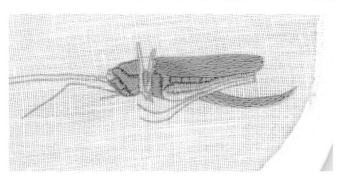

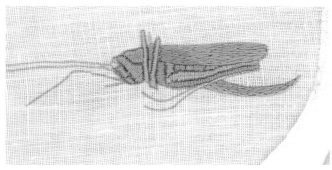

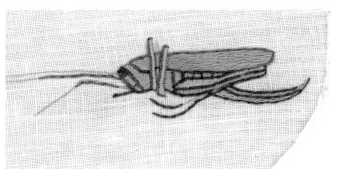

THREAD LIST
DMC
- 433
- 434
- 435
- 436
- 437
- 738
- 3021
- 3787
- 3866

ORDER OF WORK
Actual size

Step 03
738, 436; seeds 3787; frill 3866; outline 3021

Step 02a
738, 437, 436

Step 02b
738, 437, 436,
435, 434

Step 02d
436, 435,
434, 433

Step 02c
437, 436, 435,
434, 433

Step 01
738, 437,
436, 435

Outlines in
433 and 3021

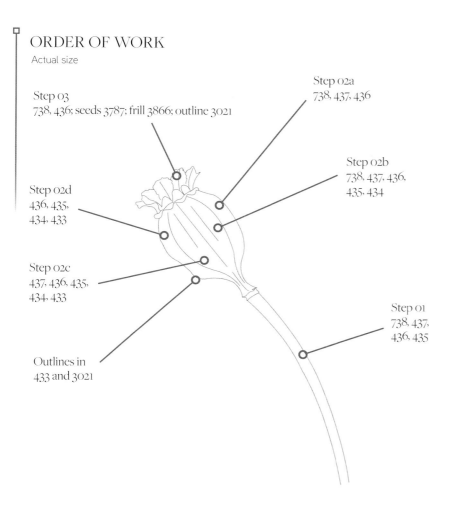

STEP 01: STEM
Fill the stem with adjacent rows of split stitch. Add horizontal bands of colour underneath the seedhead using 3866 and 3021.

STEP 02: CAPSULE
Fill each section of the pod with long-and-short stitch. Add lines in split stitch.

STEP 03: CROWN
Fill the frill with long-and-short stitch. Fill the shapes with satin stitch. Outline in split stitch.

17 ROSEHIP
ROSA

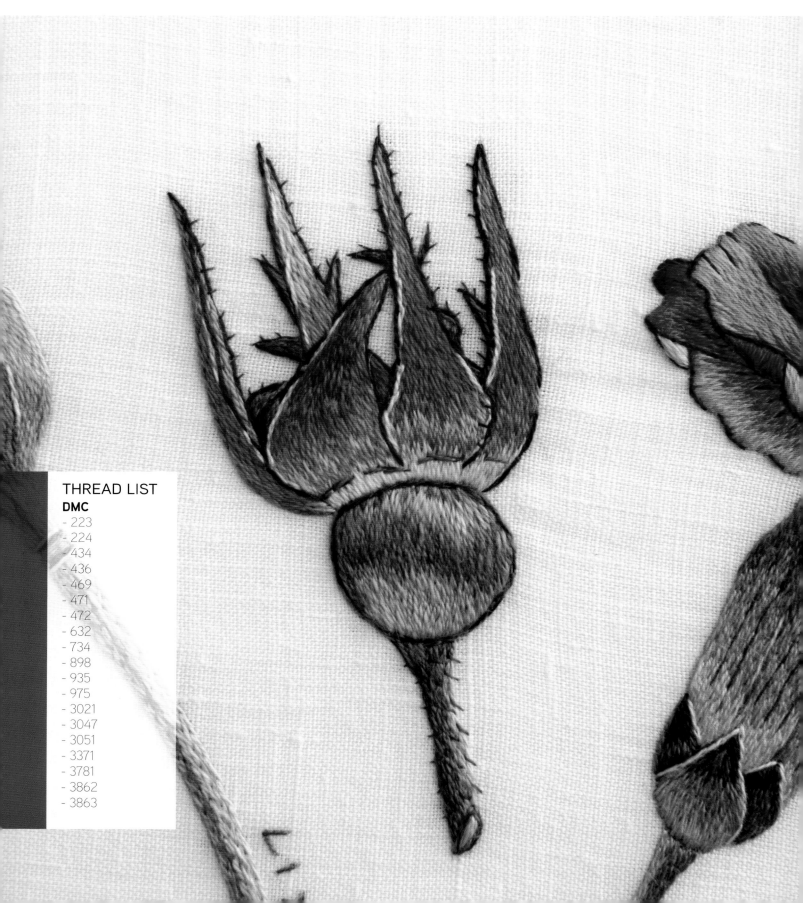

THREAD LIST

DMC
- 223
- 224
- 434
- 436
- 469
- 471
- 472
- 632
- 734
- 898
- 935
- 975
- 3021
- 3047
- 3051
- 3371
- 3781
- 3862
- 3863

ORDER OF WORK

Actual size

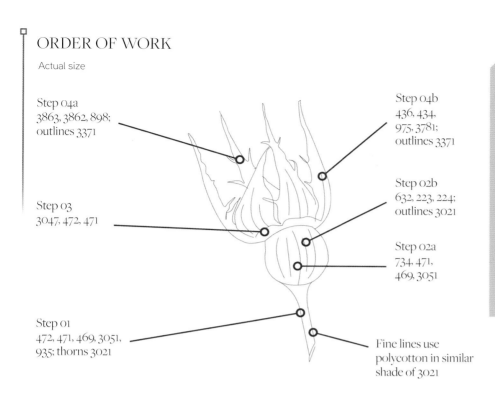

Step 04a
3863, 3862, 898;
outlines 3371

Step 04b
436, 434,
975, 3781;
outlines 3371

Step 03
3047, 472, 471

Step 02b
632, 223, 224;
outlines 3021

Step 02a
734, 471,
469, 3051

Step 01
472, 471, 469, 3051,
935; thorns 3021

Fine lines use
polycotton in similar
shade of 3021

STEP 01: STEM
Fill the stems with adjacent rows of
split stitch. Add tiny straight stitches for
the thorns.

STEP 02: HIP
Fill with long-and-short stitch; outline
in split stitch.

STEP 03: BASE OF SEPALS
Fill with long-and-short stitch.

STEP 04: SEPALS
Fill with long-and-short stitch.
Outline in split stitch. Add little spikes
in straight stitches.

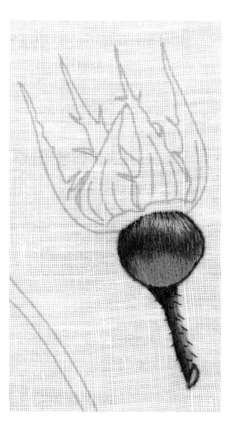

THREAD LIST

DMC	**Anchor**
Prefaced with a 'D' in the steps.	Prefaced with an 'A' in the steps.
- 320	- 31
- 368	- 36
- 501	- 41
- 502	- 42
- 989	- 43
- 3021	- 45
- 3047	- 59
- 3348	- 271
- 3362	- 968
- 3787	- 969
- Blanc	
- Fine lines: 3021 or polycotton	

ORDER OF WORK
Actual size

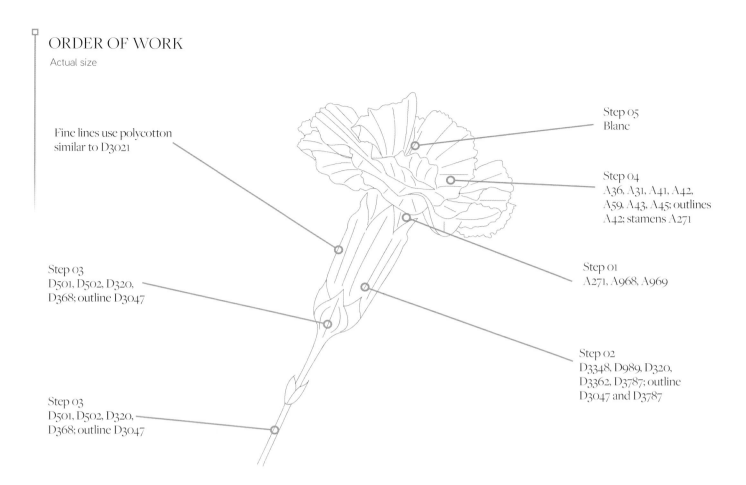

Fine lines use polycotton
similar to D3021

Step 05
Blanc

Step 04
A36, A31, A41, A42,
A59, A43, A45; outlines
A42; stamens A271

Step 03
D501, D502, D320,
D368; outline D3047

Step 01
A271, A968, A969

Step 02
D3348, D989, D320,
D3362, D3787; outline
D3047 and D3787

Step 03
D501, D502, D320,
D368; outline D3047

STEP 01: PETAL BASES
Fill with long-and-short stitch.

STEP 02: RECEPTACLE
Fill each section with long-and-short
stitch. Add lines with split stitch.

STEP 03: STEM AND SEPALS

Fill the stem and base with long-and-short stitch. Outline with split stitch.

STEP 04: PETALS

Outline each petal with split stitch, then fill with long-and-short stitch. Use the photographs as a guide for placement of colours on each petal.

STEP 05: FLOWER CENTRE

Fill the flower centre with straight stitches and a few French knots.

CLEMATIS

CLEMATIS 'MAGNIFICA'

Original illustration by Worthington G. Smith; published in
The Floral Magazine Vol. 8, 1869, from the Kew Art Collection.

THREAD LIST

DMC	- 834
- 28	- 891
- 29	- 3042
- 36	- 3051
- 319	- 3078
- 320	- 3345
- 327	- 3347
- 347	- 3348
- 367	- 3362
- 368	- 3688
- 369	- 3743
- 471	- 3801
- 498	- 3829
- 500	- 3834
- 553	- 3835
- 554	- 3836

Actual size

PROJECT SIZE

7 x 11 cm (2¾ x 4½in)

YOU WILL NEED

- Piece of fabric, 30 x 30cm (12 x 12in)
- Threads as per list, above right
- A super grip hoop or stretcher frame,
  size 20.5cm (8in)

PREPARATION

- Transfer the outline to the fabric (see pages 16 and 168).
- Mount your fabric in the hoop (see page 17).
- Follow the step-by-step instructions below and opposite.

STEP 01: STEMS
Fill the stems with adjacent rows of split stitch.

STEP 02: SMALL LEAF
Fill on either side of the leaf with long-and-short stitch.
Outline with split stitch. Fill the centre vein with split stitch.

STEP 03: BUD
Fill the bud with long-and-short stitch. Fill the centre of the bud
first with the lighter shades and then blend in the darker shades
on the sides. Add lines and outlines with split stitch.

STEP 04: LARGE LEAF
Fill on either side of the leaf with long-and-short stitch.
Outline with split stitch. Fill the centre vein with split stitch.

ORDER OF WORK

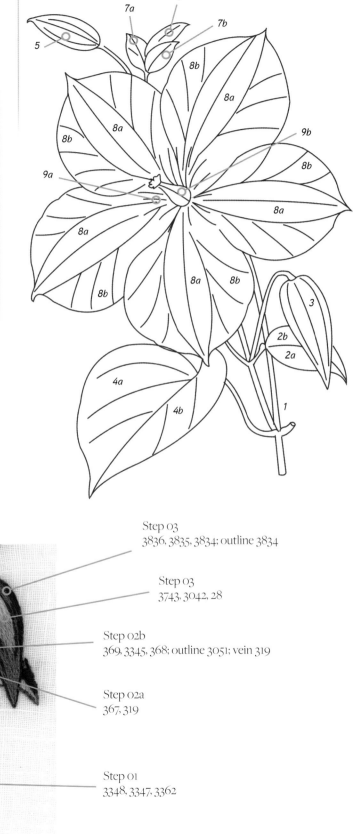

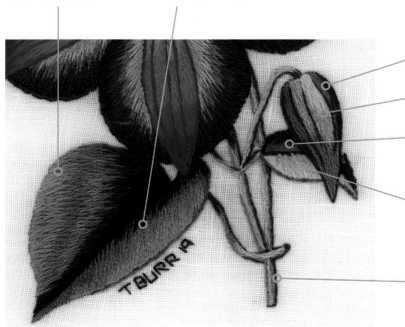

Step 04a
471, 320, 367, 319, 500

Step 04b
471, 3347, 320, 367, 319;
outline 36; vein 319

Step 03
3836, 3835, 3834; outline 3834

Step 03
3743, 3042, 28

Step 02b
369, 3345, 368; outline 3051; vein 319

Step 02a
367, 319

Step 01
3348, 3347, 3362

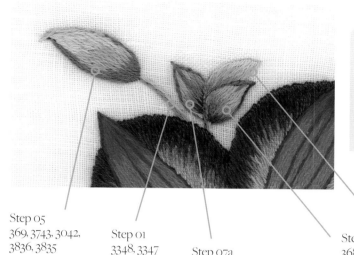

STEP 05: BUD
Fill the bud with long-and-short stitch. Outline with split stitch.

STEP 06: BUD
Fill the bud with long-and-short stitch. Outline with split stitch.

STEP 07: SMALL LEAVES
Fill the leaves with long-and-short stitch; add lines and outlines with split stitch.

Step 05
369, 3743, 3042,
3836, 3835

Step 01
3348, 3347

Step 07a
368, 320, 367; outline 3051

Step 06
3743, 3042, 3836

Step 07b
368, 320, 367; outline 3051

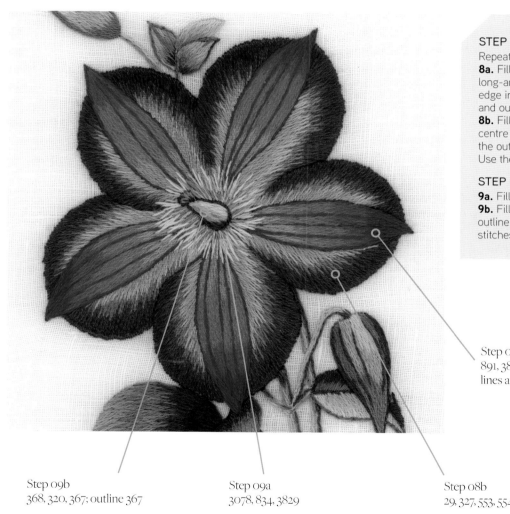

STEP 08: FLOWER PETALS
Repeat for each petal.
8a. Fill the centre of each petal with long-and-short stitch from the outside edge in towards the centre. Add lines and outlines in split stitch.
8b. Fill on either side of the red-pink centre with long-and-short stitch from the outside edge in towards the centre. Use the photograph as a guide.

STEP 09: FLOWER CENTRE
9a. Fill with straight lines.
9b. Fill with long-and-short stitch; outline with split stitch. Add tiny straight stitches at the top of the stigma.

Step 08a
891, 3801, 347, 498;
lines and outlines 498

Step 09b
368, 320, 367; outline 367

Step 09a
3078, 834, 3829

Step 08b
29, 327, 553, 554, 3688

CAMELLIA

CAMELLIA JAPONICA

Published in *Curtis's Botanical Magazine*, Vol. 2, 1788, from the Kew Art Collection.

Actual size

THREAD LIST

DMC
- 10
- 22
- 370
- 372
- 433
- 434
- 524
- 611
- 612
- 613
- 761
- 801
- 830
- 892
- 934
- 935
- 936
- 938
- 975
- 976
- 3011
- 3012
- 3013
- 3021
- 3051
- 3052
- 3053
- 3706
- 3708
- 3722
- 3801
- 3826

PROJECT SIZE

8 x 14cm (3¼ x 5½in)

YOU WILL NEED

- Piece of fabric, 30 x 30cm (12 x 12in)
- Threads as per list, above right
- A super grip hoop or stretcher frame, size 20cm (8in)

PREPARATION

- Transfer the outline to the fabric (see pages 16 and 168).
- Mount your fabric in the hoop (see page 17).
- Follow the step-by-step instructions on pages 102–105.

ORDER OF WORK

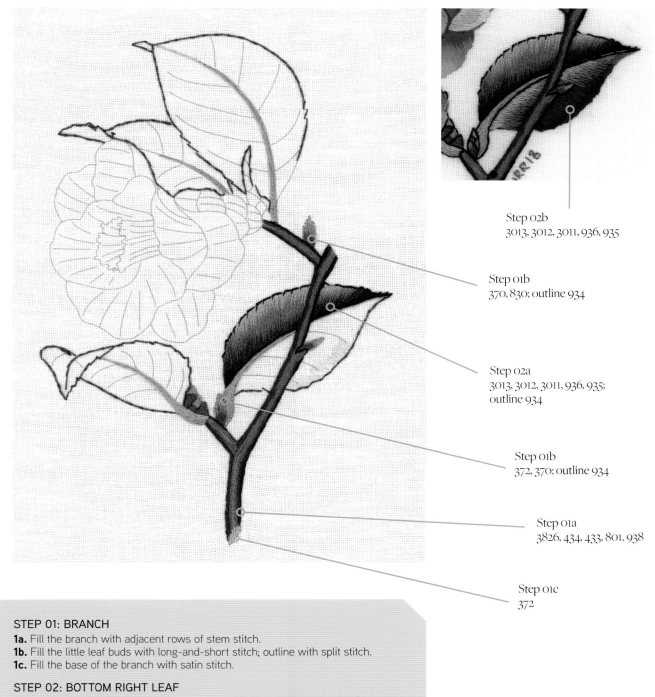

Step 02b
3013, 3012, 3011, 936, 935

Step 01b
370, 830; outline 934

Step 02a
3013, 3012, 3011, 936, 935;
outline 934

Step 01b
372, 370; outline 934

Step 01a
3826, 434, 433, 801, 938

Step 01c
372

STEP 01: BRANCH

1a. Fill the branch with adjacent rows of stem stitch.
1b. Fill the little leaf buds with long-and-short stitch; outline with split stitch.
1c. Fill the base of the branch with satin stitch.

STEP 02: BOTTOM RIGHT LEAF

2a–b. Fill each side of the leaf with long-and-short stitch, from the outside edge in towards the centre vein. Fill the centre vein with split stitch. Outline the leaf with split stitch.

STEP 03: BOTTOM LEFT LEAF

3a–b. Fill each side of the leaf with long-and-short stitch, from the outside edge in towards the centre vein. Fill the centre vein with split stitch. Outline the leaf with split stitch.

3c–d. Fill each side of the turnover with long-and-short stitch. Fill the centre vein with split stitch. Outline with split stitch.

3e. Fill each section with satin stitch; outline with split stitch.

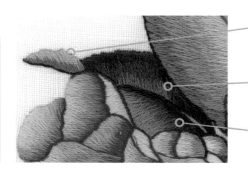

Step 03a
3013, 3012, 3011, 936;
outline 3021

Step 03b
3013, 3012, 3011; outline 3021

Step 03e
370, 830, 892;
outline 3021

Step 03c
3012, 3011, 936; outline 3021

Step 03d
3013, 3012; outline 3021

STEP 04: TOP LEFT LEAF

4a–b. Fill each side of the leaf with long-and-short stitch, from the outside edge in towards the centre vein. Fill the centre vein with split stitch. Outline the leaf with split stitch.

4c. Fill the turnover with long-and-short stitch. Outline with split stitch.

Step 04c
3013, 3012; outline 3021

Step 04a
3012, 3011, 936; outline 3021

Step 04b
3013, 3012, 3011, 936;
outline and veins 3021

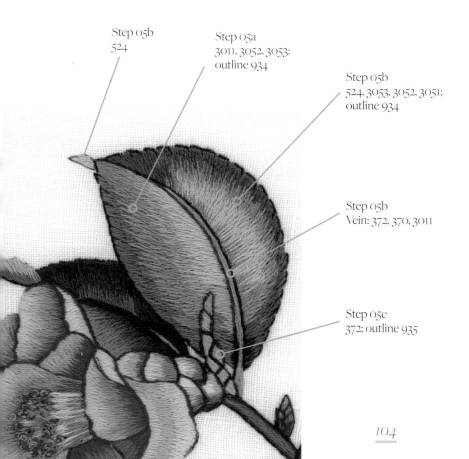

Step 05b
524

Step 05a
3011, 3052, 3053;
outline 934

Step 05b
524, 3053, 3052, 3051;
outline 934

Step 05b
Vein: 372, 370, 3011

Step 05c
372; outline 935

STEP 05: TOP RIGHT LEAF

5a–b. Fill each side of the leaf with long-and-short stitch, from the outside edge in towards the centre vein. Fill the centre vein with split stitch. Outline the leaf with split stitch. Fill the turnover with satin stitch. Outline with split stitch.

5c. Fill each section with satin stitch; outline in split stitch.

Step 06
10, 372, 3011; outline 935

STEP 06: BASE OF FLOWER
Fill each section with long-and-short stitch; outline in split stitch.

Step 07b
3708, 3706,
892, 3801, 22

Step 07c
761

Step 07d
892, 3801, 22

Step 07i
761, 3706, 3722

Step 07a
761, 3708, 3706, 892, 3722

Step 07h
761, 3708, 3706, 892, 3722

Step 08a
613, 612, 611

Step 08b
Knots 976, 975

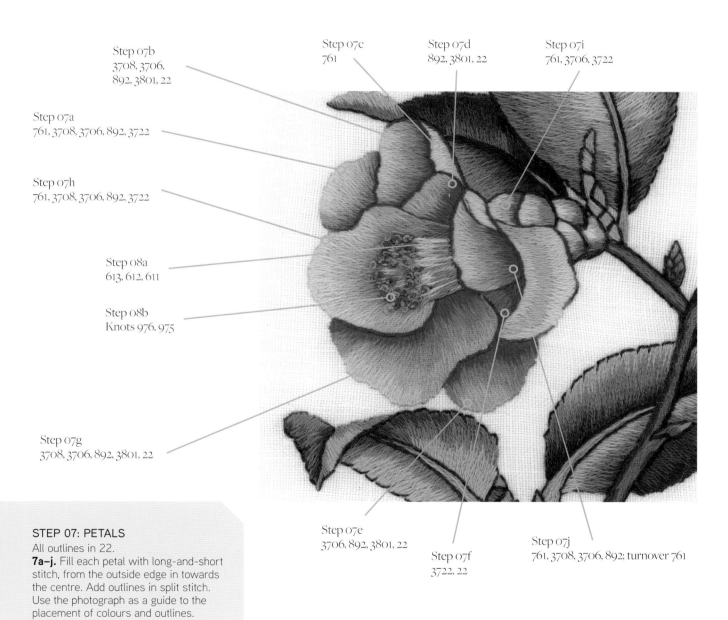

Step 07g
3708, 3706, 892, 3801, 22

Step 07e
3706, 892, 3801, 22

Step 07f
3722, 22

Step 07j
761, 3708, 3706, 892; turnover 761

STEP 07: PETALS
All outlines in 22.
7a–j. Fill each petal with long-and-short stitch, from the outside edge in towards the centre. Add outlines in split stitch. Use the photograph as a guide to the placement of colours and outlines.

STEP 08: FLOWER CENTRE
8a. Fill the filaments with straight stitch.
8b. Add French knots using one strand and two twists each time.

INTERMEDIATE PROJECTS

RHODODENDRON

RHODODENDRON THOMSONII

Original illustration by Sir Joseph Dalton Hooker, from the Kew Art Collection.

PREPARATION

- Transfer the outline to the fabric (see pages 16 and 169).
- Mount your fabric in the hoop (see page 17).
- Follow the step-by-step instructions on pages 110–115.

PROJECT SIZE

15.5 x 16.5cm (6 x 6½in)

YOU WILL NEED

- Piece of fabric, 32 x 35cm (12½ x 14in)
- Threads as per list, opposite (it is highly recommended that you use the Au Ver À Soie, Soie D'Alger silk as stated for this project, but if you have difficulty obtaining it, substitute it with DMC by using the conversion chart on page 163 – please note that the results won't be exactly the same)
- A super grip hoop or stretcher frame, size 25.5cm (10in)

Actual size

THREAD LIST

DMC
Prefaced with a
'D' in the steps.
- 2
- 3
- 7
- 8
- 10
- 165
- 355
- 471
- 500
- 520
- 543
- 645
- 646
- 734
- 801
- 920
- 976
- 3011
- 3013
- 3021
- 3364
- 3371
- 3778
- 3787
- 3799
- 3827
- 3863
- 3864
- 3866

**AVÀS Soie
D'Alger Silk**
Prefaced with an
'A' in the steps.
- 945
- 946
- 1016
- 1831
- 1832
- 1833
- 1834
- 1835
- 1836
- 1843
- 1844
- 1845
- 1846
- 2112
- 2113
- 2114
- 2922
- 2933
- 2934
- 2935
- 2943
- 3421
- 3422
- 3426
- 4623
- 4625

ORDER OF WORK

STEPS 01, 02, 03 AND 05: BRANCHES
Fill the branches with long-and-short stitch. Add lines and outlines in split stitch.

STEP 04: FINE ROOTS
Fill with split stitch in either one strand of DMC cotton or, alternatively, to achieve a very fine line, use polyester sewing cotton in similar shades.

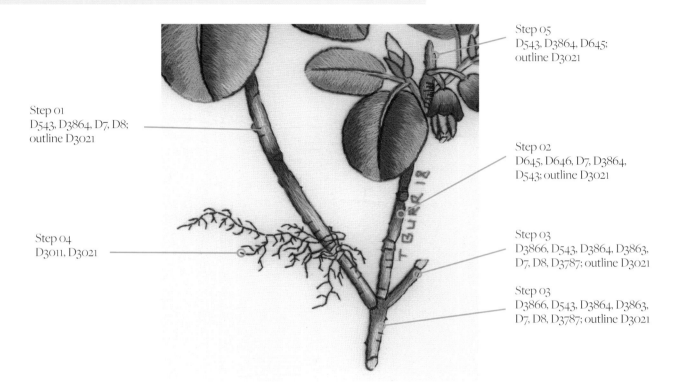

Step 05
D543, D3864, D645;
outline D3021

Step 01
D543, D3864, D7, D8;
outline D3021

Step 02
D645, D646, D7, D3864,
D543; outline D3021

Step 04
D3011, D3021

Step 03
D3866, D543, D3864, D3863,
D7, D8, D3787; outline D3021

Step 03
D3866, D543, D3864, D3863,
D7, D8, D3787; outline D3021

STEP 06: SMALL BUDS
Fill each section of the bud with padded satin stitch; outline in split stitch.

STEP 07: LARGE BUDS
7a. Fill with long-and-short stitch; outline with split stitch.
7b. Fill each section with padded satin stitch; outline with split stitch. Add straight stitches at the tip.

STEP 08: STEMS
Fill each stem with adjacent rows of split stitch; outline in split stitch.

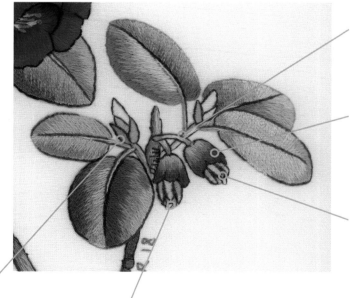

Step 08
D10, D165, D3013,
D3364, D3778;
outline D3021

Step 07a
D3827, D976, D920,
D355; outline D3021

Step 07b
D2, D3; outline
D3799

Step 06
D165, D3013, D3778; outline D3021

Step 07b
D10, D734; outline D3021

STEPS 09 AND 10: LEAVES

Fill each side of the leaf with long-and-short stitch, from the outside edge in towards the centre vein. Add the vein in split stitch. Outline in split stitch.

Step 09a
A2113, A2114, A1844;
vein D165, D520;
outlines D520

Step 09b
A2113, A2114,
A1844; vein D165,
D520; outlines D520

Step 10a
A2113, A1833, A1834,
A1845, A3426; vein D165,
D520; outlines D520, D500

Step 10b
A2113, A1833, A1834,
A1845, A3426; vein D165,
D520; outlines D520, D500

Step 13a
A1832, A1833, A1844; veins D165, D471, D520

Step 13b
A1831, A1832, A1833, A1844

Step 11a
A1831, A1832, A1833, A1844; veins D165, D471, D520

Step 11b
A1831, A1832, A1833, A1844

Step 12a
A3421, A3422, A1843; veins D165, D471, D520;
outlines D520

Step 12b
A3421, A3422, A1843

STEPS 11, 12 AND 13: LEAVES
Fill each side of each leaf with long-and-short stitch, from the outside edge in towards the centre vein. Add the vein in split stitch. Outline in split stitch.

STEPS 14, 15, 16 AND 17: LEAVES
Fill each side of each leaf with long-and-short stitch, from the outside edge in towards the centre vein. Add the veins in split stitch. Outline in split stitch.

Step 17a
A1843, A1844, A1845; vein D165, D471; outlines D3021

Step 17b
A1843, A1844, A1845; vein D165, D471; outlines D3021

Step 14a
A1835, A1836, A1846; vein D165, D471

Step 14b
A1834, A1835, A1836, A1846

Step 16b
A2113, A1833; vein D165, D471, D520; outlines D520

Step 16a
A2113, A1833, A1834; vein D165, D471, D520; outlines D520

Step 15a
A2113, A1833, A1834, A1845; vein D165, D471, D500; outlines D520

Step 15b
A2112, A2113, A1833, A1834, A1845; vein D165, D471, D500; outlines D520

STEP 18: FLOWER

Fill each section of the flower in long-and-short stitch, from the outside edge in towards the centre. Outline areas in split stitch as shown in the photograph.

STEPS 19 AND 20: FLOWERS

Fill each section of each flower in long-and-short stitch, from the outside edge in towards the centre. Fill the centre filaments with straight stitches. Add the stigmas in bullion stitches; use one strand and about ten twists for each. Outline areas in split stitch as shown in the photograph.

Step 19c
A1016, A945, A946; all outlines
D3371, D3021

Step 19d
A3422, D801, A976

Step 19a
A2113, A2114, A2933, A1016;
outline D3021

Step 20a
A1016, A945, A946; outlines
D3371, D3021

Step 19b
A2943, A2934,
A945, A4623

Step 20c
A3422, D801, D976

Step 18b
A2933, A2934, A2935, A946;
outlines D3371, D3021

Step 20b
A946, A4625

Step 18a
A945, A946

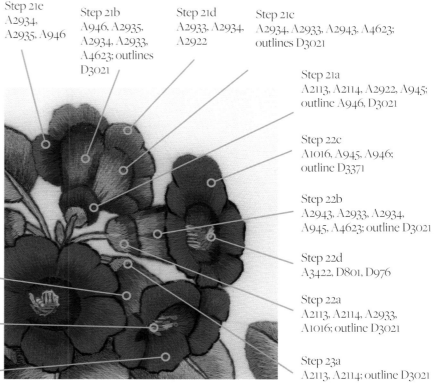

STEP 21: FLOWER

Fill each section of the flower in long-and-short stitch, from the outside edge in towards the centre. Outline areas in split stitch as shown in the photograph.

STEPS 22 AND 23: FLOWERS

Fill each section of each flower in long-and-short stitch, from the outside edge in towards the centre. Fill the centre filaments with straight stitches; add the stigmas in bullion stitches, using one strand and about ten twists for each. Outline areas in split stitch as shown in the photograph.

Step 21e
A2934,
A2935, A946

Step 21b
A946, A2935,
A2934, A2933,
A4623; outlines
D3021

Step 21d
A2933, A2934,
A2922

Step 21c
A2934, A2933, A2943, A4623;
outlines D3021

Step 21a
A2113, A2114, A2922, A945;
outline A946, D3021

Step 22c
A1016, A945, A946;
outline D3371

Step 22b
A2943, A2933, A2934,
A945, A4623; outline D3021

Step 23b
A946, A2935, A2934,
A2933, A4623; outline D3021

Step 22d
A3422, D801, D976

Step 23d
A3422, D801, D976

Step 22a
A2113, A2114, A2933,
A1016; outline D3021

Step 23c
A1016, A945, A946; outline D3371

Step 23a
A2113, A2114; outline D3021

WATERLILY

NYMPHAEA CAERULEA

Original illustration by Pierre-Joseph Redouté, from the Kew Art Collection.

PROJECT SIZE

13 x 20cm (5 x 8in)

YOU WILL NEED

- Piece of fabric, 32 x 35cm (12½ x 14in)
- Threads as per list, opposite
- A super grip hoop or stretcher frame, size 25.5cm (10in)

Actual size

THREAD LIST

DMC
Prefaced with a
'D' in the steps.
- 10
- 11
- 25
- 26
- 27
- 156
- 341
- 500
- 632
- 734
- 792
- 934
- 935
- 3021
- 3064
- 3772
- 3787
- 3807

**AVÀS Soie
D'Alger Silk**
Prefaced with
an 'A' in the
steps.
- 2133
- 3425
- 3426
- 3712
- 3713
- 3714
- 3715
- 3716
- 3724
- 3832
- 3833
- 3834
- 3835
- 3836
- 3841
- 3843
- 3844
- 3845
- 5022
- 5023
- 5024

It is highly recommended that you
use the Au Ver à Soie, Soie D'Alger
silk as stated for this project, but
if you have difficulty obtaining it,
substitute it with DMC by using the
conversion chart on page 163 –
please note that the results will not
be exactly the same.

PREPARATION

- Transfer the outline to the fabric (see pages 16 and 170).
- Mount your fabric in the hoop (see page 17).
- Follow the step-by-step instructions on pages 118–120.

ORDER OF WORK

STEP 01: STEMS

1a–f. Fill all the stems with adjacent rows of split stitch, using one strand of each colour. Add outlines in split stitch along one or both sides; use the photograph as a guide to placement of shades. Please note: stems 1d and 1e have different shades on the tops and bottoms of the stems.

Step 01b
A3845, A3844, A3843, A3841;
outline D935

Step 01e
A3845, A3844, A3843,
A3841; outline D935

Step 01d
A3832, A3833, A3834, A3835,
A3836; outline D3787

Step 01c
A3713, A3714, A3715, A3716;
outline D935 and D3021

Step 01d
A3712, A3713, A3714, A3715,
A3835, A3836; outline D3787

Step 01a
D3064, D3772, D632, D3787

Step 01c
A3845, A3844, A3843,
A3841, A3713, A3712

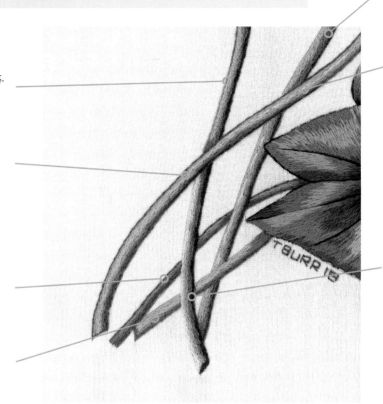

STEP 02: BUDS

2a–b. Fill both buds with long-and-short stitch, from the tip towards the base. On bud 2a add a bit of satin stitch at the base. Outline the buds in split stitch in D934.

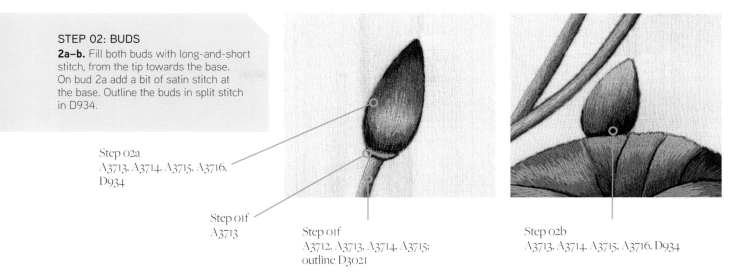

Step 02a
A3713, A3714, A3715, A3716, D934

Step 01f
A3713

Step 01f
A3712, A3713, A3714, A3715;
outline D3021

Step 02b
A3713, A3714, A3715, A3716, D934

STEP 03: LARGE LEAF

Fill each section of the leaf (between the veins) with long-and-short stitch, from the outside edge in towards the centre. Add veins and outlines with split stitch in D500. If in doubt as to the placement of colours for each section, check the thread colours and refer to the photograph as a guide.

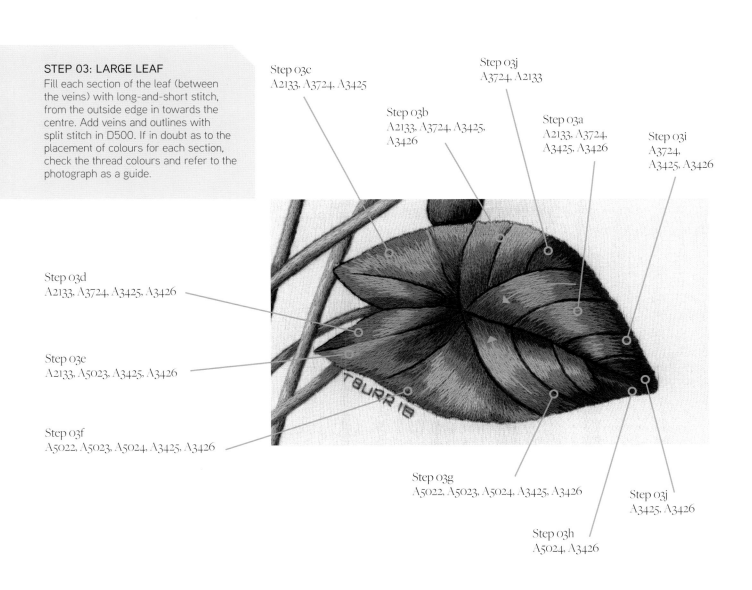

Step 03c
A2133, A3724, A3425

Step 03j
A3724, A2133

Step 03b
A2133, A3724, A3425, A3426

Step 03a
A2133, A3724, A3425, A3426

Step 03i
A3724, A3425, A3426

Step 03d
A2133, A3724, A3425, A3426

Step 03e
A2133, A5023, A3425, A3426

Step 03f
A5022, A5023, A5024, A3425, A3426

Step 03g
A5022, A5023, A5024, A3425, A3426

Step 03j
A3425, A3426

Step 03h
A5024, A3426

STEP 04: LEFT-HAND WATERLILY
Fill the petals with long-and-short stitch, from the tip down towards the base; outline with split stitch.

STEP 05: LEFT-HAND WATERLILY LEAVES
Fill the leaves with long-and-short stitch, from the tip down towards the base; outline with split stitch.

STEP 06: WATERLILY CENTRES
Add straight stitches at the base of the petal. Fill the filaments with split stitch. Fill the anthers with French knots using one strand and two twists.

Step 06
Anthers D3807, D26

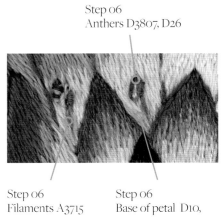

Step 06
Filaments A3715

Step 06
Base of petal D10, D11, D734

Step 05c
A3713, A3714

Step 04b
D3807, D156, D26; outline D792

Step 05b
A3714, A3715, A3716; outline D934

Step 05a
A3713, A3714, A3715, A3716; outline D935 and D934

Step 04a
D3807, D156, D26, D25, D27; outline D792

Step 04c
D792, D3807, D156, D26, D25, D10, D11; outline D792

Step 05b
A3714, A3715, A3716; outline D934

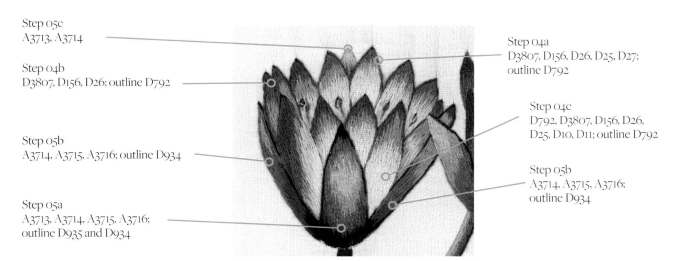

STEP 07: RIGHT-HAND WATERLILY
Fill the petals with long-and-short stitch, from the tip down towards the base. Outline with split stitch.

STEP 08: RIGHT-HAND WATERLILY LEAVES
Fill the leaves with long-and-short stitch, from the tip down towards the base; outline with split stitch.

Step 07b
D3807, D156, D341; outline D792

Step 07a
D3807, D156, D341, D26, D25, D27; outline D792

See step 06, above

Step 07a
D3807, D156, D341, D26, D25, D27; outline D792

Step 07b
D3807, D156, D341, D26; outline D792

Step 07b
D3807, D156, D341, D26; outline D792

Step 08a
A3713, A3714, A3715, A3716; outline D935 and D934

Step 07c
D792, D3807, D156, D341, D26, D10, D734; outline D792

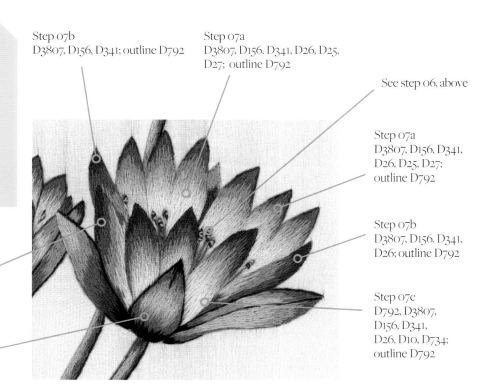

Actual size

アヤメ

IRIS

IRIS SANGUINEA

Original woodblock print on paper, 1828, from *Honzo Zufu* (Illustrated manual of medicinal plants) by Kan'en Iwasaki from the Kew Art Collection.

PREPARATION

- Transfer the outline to the fabric (see pages 16 and 171).
- Mount your fabric in the hoop (see page 17).
- Follow the step-by-step instructions on pages 124–127.

ORDER OF WORK

アヤメ

THREAD LIST

DMC	AVÀS Soie D'Alger Silk
Prefaced with a 'D' in the steps.	Prefaced with an 'A' in the steps.
- 310	- 112
- 632	- 242
- 935	- 532
- 3772	- 1341
- 3787	- 1342
- Blanc	- 1343
	- 1344
	- 1345
	- 1426
	- 1721
	- 1842
	- 1843
	- 1844
	- 1845
	- 1846
	- 2132
	- 2133
	- 2134
	- 2135
	- 3732
	- 3733
	- 3734
	- 4213
	- 4214
	- 4913
	- 4914
	- 4915
	- 4916

It is highly recommended that you use the Au Ver à Soie, Soie D'Alger silk as stated for this project, but if you have difficulty obtaining it, substitute it with DMC by using the conversion chart on page 163 – please note that the results will not be exactly the same.

PROJECT SIZE

14 x 24cm (5½ x 9½in)

YOU WILL NEED

- Piece of fabric, 32 x 35cm (12½ x 14in)
- Threads as per list, above
- A super grip hoop or stretcher frame, size 25.5cm (10in)

STEP 01: ALL STEMS AND LEAVES

Fill the stems and leaves with long-and-short stitch. Use the photograph as a guide to the placement of colours and shading.

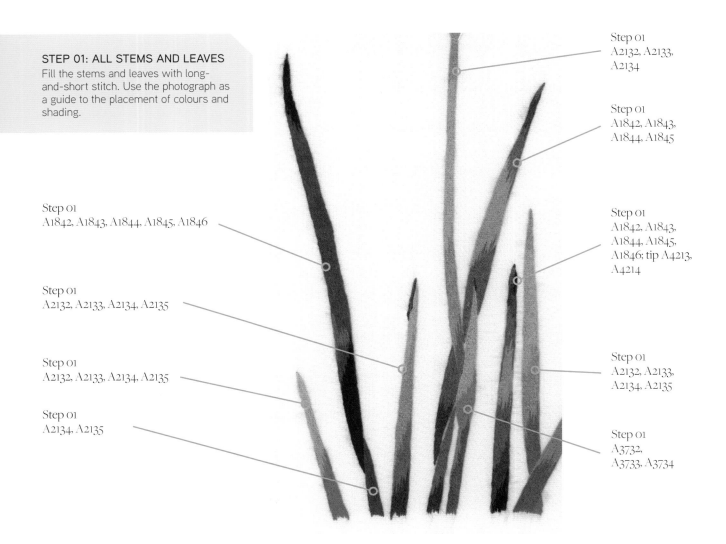

Step 01
A2132, A2133, A2134

Step 01
A1842, A1843, A1844, A1845

Step 01
A1842, A1843, A1844, A1845, A1846; tip A4213, A4214

Step 01
A1842, A1843, A1844, A1845, A1846

Step 01
A2132, A2133, A2134, A2135

Step 01
A2132, A2133, A2134, A2135

Step 01
A2134, A2135

Step 01
A2132, A2133, A2134, A2135

Step 01
A3732, A3733, A3734

STEP 02: SEPALS

Fill the sepals with long-and-short stitch. Add lines in split stitch. Add a white dividing outline in blanc, in split stitch, as shown in the photograph.

Step 02
D3772, D632;
outlines D935 and blanc

Step 02
A2133, A2134, A1844, A3734

STEPS 03–09: PETALS

Fill all the petals with long-and-short stitch. Add white outlines in blanc, in split stitch, as shown.

Step 03
A1343, A1344, A1345

Step 04
A1343, A1344

Step 05
A1344, A1345, A1426

Step 06
A4914, A4915, A4916, A1345

Step 07
A1342, A1343, A1344, A1345, A1426

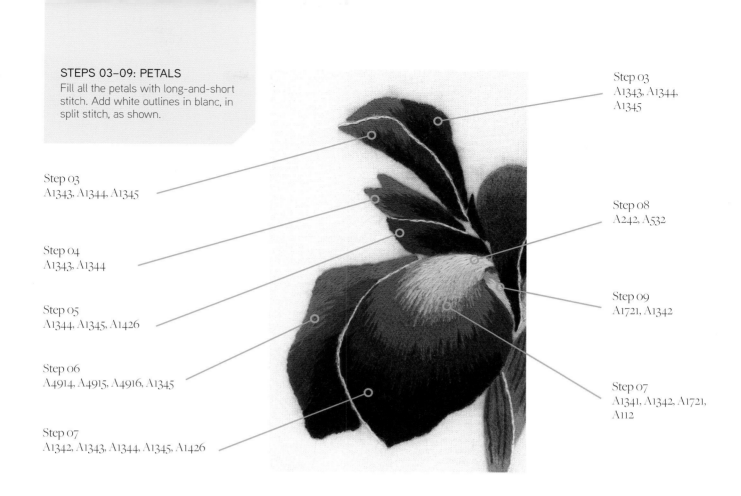

Step 03
A1343, A1344, A1345

Step 08
A242, A532

Step 09
A1721, A1342

Step 07
A1341, A1342, A1721, A112

STEPS 10–18: PETALS

Fill all the petals with long-and-short stitch. Add white outlines in blanc, in split stitch, as shown in the photograph.

STEP 19: SIGNATURE

The signature is one of the words for *Iris* in Japanese. Fill the signature with split stitch in D310 (black).

Step 012
A4913, A4914, A4915, A4916, A1345

Step 13
A1344, A1345, A1426

Step 15
A1721, A1341, A1342; outline D3787

Step 18
A1426

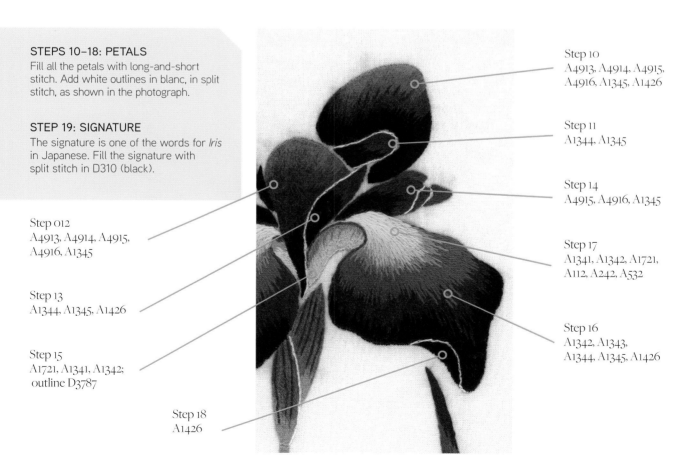

Step 10
A4913, A4914, A4915, A4916, A1345, A1426

Step 11
A1344, A1345

Step 14
A4915, A4916, A1345

Step 17
A1341, A1342, A1721, A112, A242, A532

Step 16
A1342, A1343, A1344, A1345, A1426

Actual size

SPIDER CHRYSANTHEMUM

DENDRANTHEMA

Original woodblock print on paper, 1828, from *Honzo Zufu* (Illustrated manual of medicinal plants) by Kan'en Iwasaki from the Kew Art Collection.

THREAD LIST

DMC	AVÀS Soie D'Alger Silk
Prefaced with a 'D' in the steps.	Prefaced with an 'A' in the steps.
- 09	- 1832
- 310	- 1833
- 500	- 1842
- 501	- 1843
- 3860	- 1844
	- 1845
	- 2122
	- 2132
	- 2133
	- 2134
	- 2135
	- 2926
	- 2941
	- 3011
	- 3733
	- 3734
	- 4147
	- 4622
	- 4623
	- 4624

It is highly recommended that you use the Au Ver à Soie, Soie D'Alger silk as stated for this project, but if you have difficulty obtaining it, substitute it with DMC by using the conversion chart on page 163 – please note that the results will not be exactly the same.

PROJECT SIZE

17.5 x 23.5cm (7 x 9½in)

YOU WILL NEED

- Piece of fabric, 32 x 35cm (12½ x 14in)
- Threads as per list, left
- A super grip hoop or stretcher frame, size 25.5cm (10in)

ORDER OF WORK

PREPARATION

- Transfer the outline to the fabric (see pages 16 and 172).
- Mount your fabric in the hoop (see page 17).
- Follow the step-by-step instructions on pages 131–132.

STEP 01: STEMS

Fill the stems with adjacent rows of split stitch. Use the photograph as a guide to the placement of colours.

STEP 02: LEAF

Fill either side of the leaf in long-and-short stitch, from the outside edge in towards the centre vein. Fill the lines and veins with split stitch.

STEP 03: LEAF

3a–3b. Fill either side of the leaf in long-and-short stitch, from the outside edge in towards the centre vein. Fill the lines and veins with split stitch.

3c. Fill the small leaves with long-and-short stitch or satin stitch. Add the lines in split stitch.

STEP 04: LEAF

4a–4b. Fill either side of the leaf in long-and-short stitch, from the outside edge in towards the centre vein. Fill the lines and veins with split stitch.

4c. Fill the small leaves with long-and-short stitch or satin stitch. Add the lines in split stitch.

STEP 05: LEAF

Fill either side of the leaf in long-and-short stitch, from the outside edge in towards the centre vein. Fill the lines and veins with split stitch.

STEP 06: SMALL LEAVES

Fill the leaves with long-and-short stitch; add outlines in split stitch.

Step 05a
A1843, A1844;
veins D500

Step 06
A2132, A2133,
A2134; veins
D501

Step 05b
A1843, A1844;
veins D500

Step 03b
A1842, A1843,
A1844, A1845;
veins D500

Step 04a
A1832, A1833,
A1844; veins
D500

Step 03a
A1832, A1833,
A1844, A1845;
veins D500

Step 04b
A1843, A1844, A1845;
veins D500

Step 04c
A2132, A2133, A3733, A3734;
veins D500

Step 02a
A1832, A1833,
A1844, A1845;
veins D500

Step 02b
A1842, A1843,
A1844, A1845;
veins D500

Step 01
A2122, A2133,
A2134, A2135

Step 03c
A2132, A2133,
A2135, A3733,
A3734; veins D500

Step 12
D310

STEP 07: SMALL LEAVES
Fill the leaves with long-and-short stitch.
Add lines in split stitch.

STEP 08: BUD
Fill the bud with long-and-short stitch
and the sepals with satin stitch. Add
outlines in split stitch.

STEP 09: SEPALS
Fill the sepals with long-and-short stitch;
add outlines in split stitch.

STEP 10: SMALL FLOWER
Fill each petal with long-and-short stitch,
from the tip towards the base; outline with
split stitch. Refer to the photograph for
the placement of shades.

STEP 11: LARGE FLOWER
Fill each petal with long-and-short stitch,
from the tip towards the centre. Add
some outlines in split stitch – refer to the
photograph for petals that are outlined.
Fill the dark tips with long-and-short
stitch; outline in split stitch.

STEP 12: SIGNATURE
Fill with adjacent rows of split stitch.

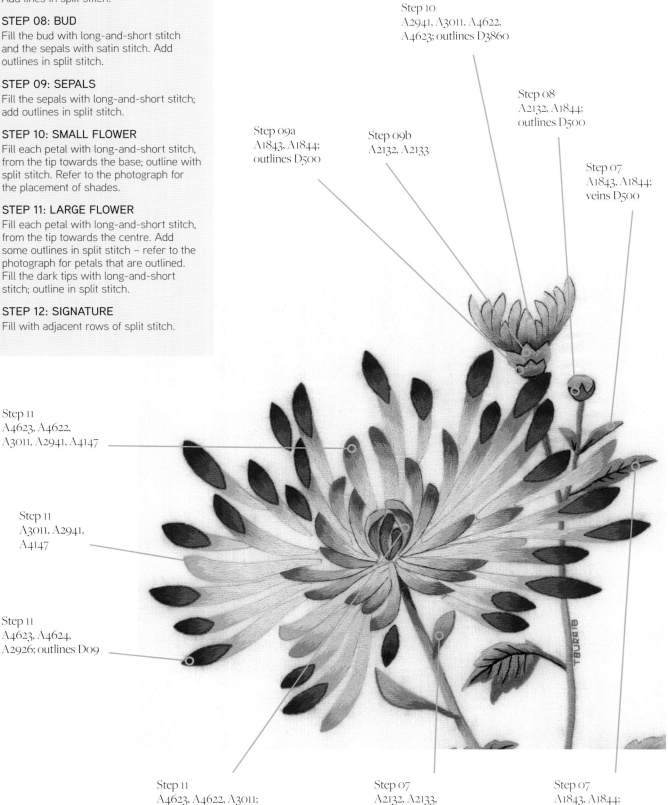

Step 10
A2941, A3011, A4622,
A4623; outlines D3860

Step 08
A2132, A1844;
outlines D500

Step 09a
A1843, A1844;
outlines D500

Step 09b
A2132, A2133

Step 07
A1843, A1844;
veins D500

Step 11
A4623, A4622,
A3011, A2941, A4147

Step 11
A3011, A2941,
A4147

Step 11
A4623, A4624,
A2926; outlines D09

Step 11
A4623, A4622, A3011;
outline D3860

Step 07
A2132, A2133,
A2134; veins D501

Step 07
A1843, A1844;
veins D500

papaver

ADVANCED
PROJECTS

ROSE

ROSA GALLICA 'VERSICOLOR'

Original illustration by Pierre-Joseph Redouté, from the Kew Art Collection.

PREPARATION

- Transfer the outline to the fabric (see pages 16 and 173).
- Mount your fabric in the hoop (see page 17).
- Follow the step-by-step instructions on pages 140–143; use one strand of thread unless specified otherwise.

PROJECT SIZE
13.5 x 14.5cm (5½ x 5¾in)

YOU WILL NEED
- Piece of fabric, 32 x 32cm (12¾ x 12¾in)
- Threads as per list, opposite
- A super grip hoop, size 20cm (8in)

Actual size

THREAD LIST

DMC
Prefaced with a 'D'
in the steps.
- 09
- 152
- 221
- 223
- 224
- 225
- 452
- 453
- 471
- 500
- 501
- 680
- 727
- 729
- 869
- 935
- 3078
- 3348
- 3721
- 3722
- 3860
- 3861
- 3865
- Blanc

Anchor
Prefaced with an 'A'
in the steps.
- 213
- 214
- 215
- 216
- 267
- 268

ORDER OF WORK

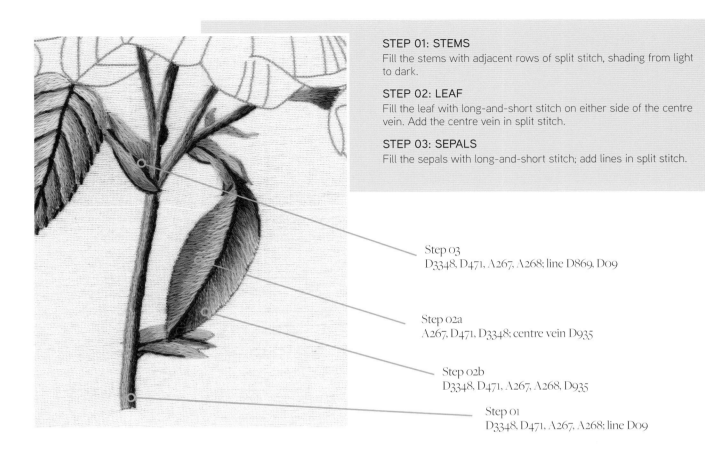

STEP 01: STEMS
Fill the stems with adjacent rows of split stitch, shading from light to dark.

STEP 02: LEAF
Fill the leaf with long-and-short stitch on either side of the centre vein. Add the centre vein in split stitch.

STEP 03: SEPALS
Fill the sepals with long-and-short stitch; add lines in split stitch.

Step 03
D3348, D471, A267, A268; line D869, D09

Step 02a
A267, D471, D3348; centre vein D935

Step 02b
D3348, D471, A267, A268, D935

Step 01
D3348, D471, A267, A268; line D09

STEPS 04, 05 AND 06: LEAVES
Start by filling in the veins with split stitch. Fill the sections between the veins with long-and-short stitch. Work one side of the leaf and then the other on either side of the centre vein. Go back over the veins with split stitch to define them. Add little spikes in straight stitches at the edges of the leaves in D501. Add the centre veins in split stitch.

STEP 07: LEAF
Fill the leaf as for the others, adjusting to fit and leaving out the spikes.

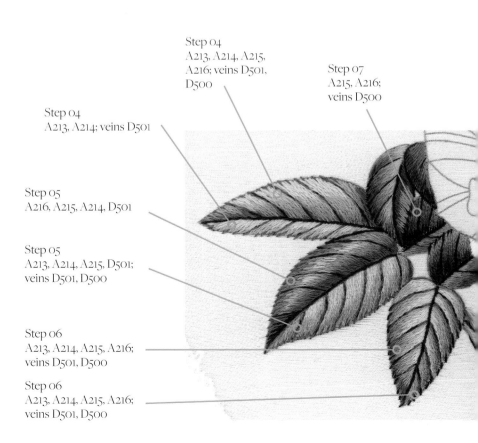

Step 04
A213, A214, A215, A216; veins D501, D500

Step 07
A215, A216; veins D500

Step 04
A213, A214; veins D501

Step 05
A216, A215, A214, D501

Step 05
A213, A214, A215, D501; veins D501, D500

Step 06
A213, A214, A215, A216; veins D501, D500

Step 06
A213, A214, A215, A216; veins D501, D500

Step 09
A267, A268; veins D500

Step 09
D3348, D471, A267, A268;
veins D500

Step 09
D471, A268; veins D500

Step 08
A267, A268, D501;
veins D500

Step 08
A267, A268; veins D500

STEPS 08 AND 09: LEAVES

Start by filling in the veins with split stitch. Fill the sections between the veins with long-and-short stitch. Work one side of the leaf and then the other on either side of the centre vein. Go back over the veins with split stitch to define them. Add little spikes in straight stitches at the edge of the leaf in D501. Add the centre vein in split stitch.

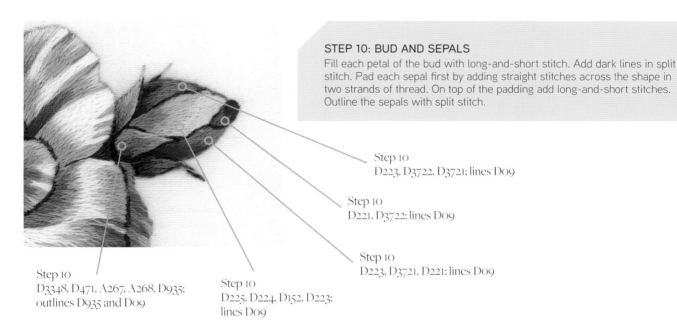

STEP 10: BUD AND SEPALS

Fill each petal of the bud with long-and-short stitch. Add dark lines in split stitch. Pad each sepal first by adding straight stitches across the shape in two strands of thread. On top of the padding add long-and-short stitches. Outline the sepals with split stitch.

Step 10
D223, D3722, D3721; lines D09

Step 10
D221, D3722; lines D09

Step 10
D223, D3721, D221; lines D09

Step 10
D3348, D471, A267, A268, D935;
outlines D935 and D09

Step 10
D225, D224, D152, D223;
lines D09

STEPS 11 AND 12:
BUD AND SEPALS

Fill each section of the bud with long-and-short stitch or satin stitch where space does not allow. Outline the petals with split stitch in D09.
Pad the sepals first by adding straight stitches across the shape in two strands of thread. On top of this add long-and-short stitch. Add the outlines in split stitch in D09.

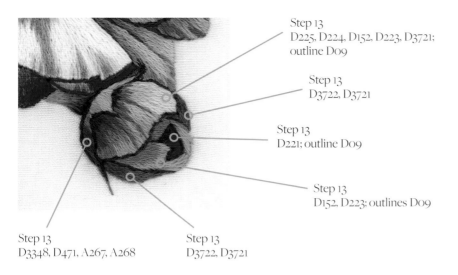

Step 13
D225, D224, D152, D223, D3721;
outline D09

Step 13
D3722, D3721

Step 13
D221; outline D09

Step 13
D152, D223; outlines D09

Step 13
D3348, D471, A267, A268

Step 13
D3722, D3721

STEP 13: BUD AND SEPALS

Fill each section of the bud with long-and-short stitch or satin stitch where space does not allow. Outline the petals with split stitch. Stitch the sepals in long-and-short stitch. Add the lines and outlines in split stitch in D09.

STEP 14: ROSE PETALS

Start with the petals that are furthest back and work towards the petals at the front. Outline each petal with split stitch in two strands. Fill each petal with long-and-short stitch, from the outside edge in towards the centre. Ensure that you cover the split stitch outlines. Refer to the photographs for colour placement in each petal – you will need to change the shades to include the variegated areas (stripes) or, if preferred, you can add these in afterwards. Add outlines in split stitch to define in D09 and D3721.

Step 14
Blanc, D3865, D225, D152, D223, D3722, D3721, D452, D453

Step 14
Blanc, D3865, D225, D152

Step 14
Blanc, D3865, D225, D152

Step 14
D452, D3860

Step 14
D3865, D225

Step 14
D3865, D225, D152, D223, D3722, D3721, D452

Step 14
D452, D3861, D3860

Step 14
D453, D452, D3865, D152, D223, D3722, D3721, D221

Step 14
Blanc, D3865, D225, D152, D223, D3722, D3721

Step 14
D452, D453, D3865, D3861, D3860

Step 14
D3722, D3721, D221

Step 14
D3721, D223, D152, D225, D3865

Step 14
D3861, D3860, D3722, D152

Step 14
Blanc, D3865, D225, D152, D223, D3722, D3721

Step 14
D453, D452, D3861, D3860

Step 14
Blanc, D3865, D225, D152, D223, D3722

Step 14
Blanc, D3865, D452

Step 14
Blanc, D225, D224, D3722, D3721, D221

Step 14
Blanc, D3865, D453, D452, D152, D3861

Step 14
D152, D3722, D221

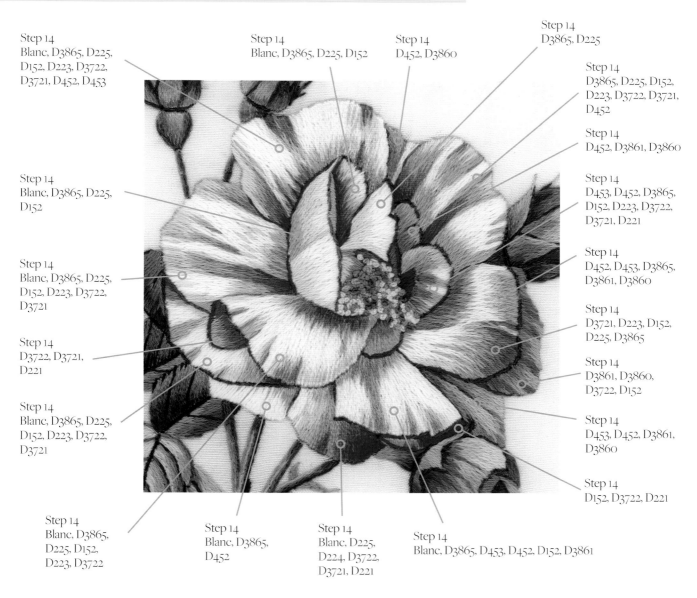

STEP 15: ROSE CENTRE

Add French knots in the centre. Use two strands and one twist of each colour.

Step 15
D680, D729, D727, D3078

143

MAGNOLIA

MAGNOLIA GRANDIFLORA

Original illustration by Georg Dionysius Ehret, from the
Kew Art Collection.

PREPARATION

- Transfer the outline to the fabric (see pages 16 and 174).
- Mount your fabric in the hoop (see page 17).
- Follow the step-by-step instructions on pages 146–153.

PROJECT SIZE

12.5 x 16cm (5 x 6¼in)

YOU WILL NEED

- Piece of fabric, 32 x 35cm (12¾ x 13¾in)
- Threads as per list, opposite
- A super grip hoop, size 20cm (8in)

Actual size

THREAD LIST

DMC
Prefaced with a 'D'
in the steps.
- 310
- 433
- 471
- 472
- 500
- 520
- 645
- 646
- 732
- 830
- 927
- 934
- 935
- 3011
- 3021
- 3051
- 3052
- 3053
- 3363
- 3787

**AVÀS Soie
D'Alger Silk**
Prefaced with an 'A'
in the steps.
- 531
- 2232
- 3221
- 3222
- 3224
- 3421
- 3442
- 3712
- 3713
- 3814
- 3832
- 3841
- 3842
- 3843
- 3844
- 3845
- 3846
- 4096
- 4102
- 4104
- Blanc

It is recommended that you
use the Au Ver à Soie, Soie
D'Alger silk as stated, but if
you have difficulty obtaining it,
substitute it with DMC using the
conversion chart on page 163
– please note that the results
won't be exactly the same.

ORDER OF WORK

STEP 01: STEM
Fill the stem with long-and-short stitch or adjacent lines of split stitches. Fill the notches with satin stitch. Add the outlines in split stitch or straight stitches, using the photograph as a guide.

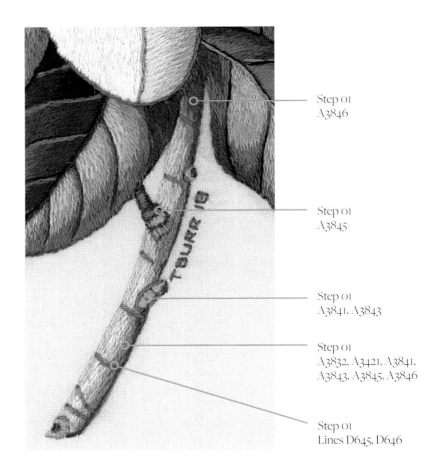

Step 01
A3846

Step 01
A3845

Step 01
A3841, A3843

Step 01
A3832, A3421, A3841,
A3843, A3845, A3846

Step 01
Lines D645, D646

STEP 02: LEAF

Pad each section of the leaf. Fill each side of the leaf with long-and-short stitch. Add the veins in split stitch.

STEP 03: LEAF

Pad each section of the leaf. Fill each side of the leaf with long-and-short stitch. Add the veins in split stitch.

STEP 04: LEAF

Pad each section of the leaf. Fill each side of the leaf with long-and-short stitch. Add the veins in split stitch.

STEP 05: SMALL LEAF

Fill the small leaf with adjacent rows of split stitch.

PADDING LEAVES

You will need to pad each section of the leaf before filling with long-and-short stitch. To do this, use two strands of a medium shade of green and add straight stitches across the shape. Leave little gaps for the veins. The padding raises the area; the long-and-short stitch will be worked on top of this.

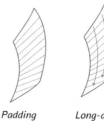

Padding   *Long-and-short stitch*

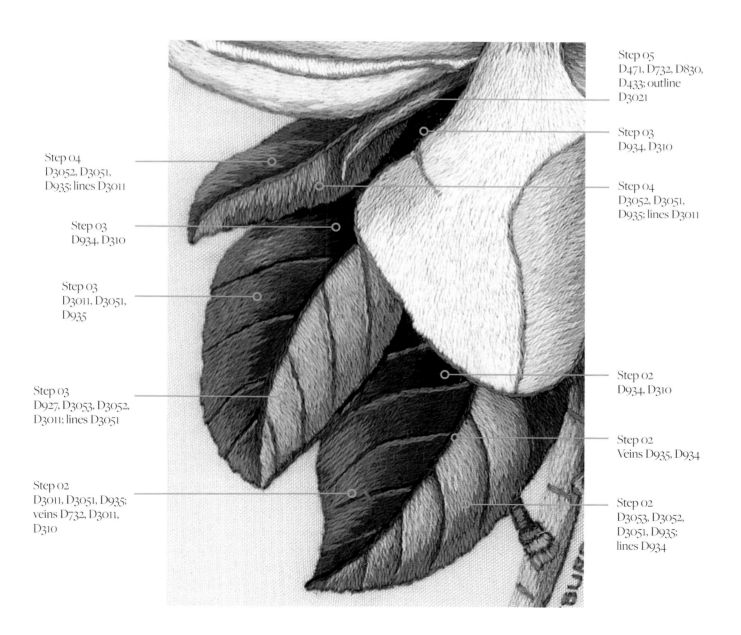

Step 05
D471, D732, D830, D433; outline D3021

Step 03
D934, D310

Step 04
D3052, D3051, D935; lines D3011

Step 04
D3052, D3051, D935; lines D3011

Step 03
D934, D310

Step 03
D3011, D3051, D935

Step 03
D927, D3053, D3052, D3011; lines D3051

Step 02
D934, D310

Step 02
Veins D935, D934

Step 02
D3011, D3051, D935; veins D732, D3011, D310

Step 02
D3053, D3052, D3051, D935; lines D934

STEP 06: LEAF

Pad each section of the leaf (see page 147). Fill each side of the leaf with long-and-short stitch. Add the veins in split stitch.

STEP 07: LEAF

Pad each section of the leaf on the right side only, not the left. Fill each side of the leaf with long-and-short stitch. Add the veins in split stitch. Add highlights on top of previous stitching.

STEP 08: LEAF

Pad each section of the leaf. Fill each side of the leaf with long-and-short stitch. Add the veins in split stitch.

STEP 09: SMALL LEAF

Fill the small leaf with adjacent rows of split stitch. Fill the vein with split stitch. Add outlines in split stitch.

Step 09
D472, D471, D732, D830, D433; outline D3021

Step 07
Shadows D934, D310

Step 07
D3052, D3051, D935, D934, D310; lines D310

Step 08
D520, D500, D310; lines D310 and D3011

Step 08
D520, D500, D310; lines D310 and D3011

Step 07
Shadows D935, D934, D310

Step 07
Highlight D927

Step 07
D3052, D3051, D935; lines D3011, D934

Step 06
D3011, D3052, D3051, D935, D934; lines D934, D310, D3052

Step 06
D3053, D3052, D3051, D935, D934; lines D3011, D310

STEPS 10–13: LEAVES

Fill in either side of the leaf with long-and-short stitch. Add the veins in split stitch. Please note that these leaves are in the background, so do not need to be padded.

Step 11
D520, D500; lines
D3011, D310

Step 11
D3363, D520,
D500; lines
D3011, D310

Step 10
D3363, D520, D500; lines D3011, D310

Step 13
D3053, D3052, D3051,
D935, D934

Step 12
D3053, D3052, D3051, D935

STEP 14: PETAL

Outline the petal with split stitch in A3221. Fill the petal with long-and-short stitch, from the outside edge in towards the centre. Fill the turnover with padded satin stitch. Outline all in split stitch.

STEP 15: PETAL

Outline the petal with split stitch in A3221. Fill the inside of the petal with long-and-short stitch, from the outside edge in towards the centre. Fill the petal underside with long-and-short stitch. Fill the small turnover with padded satin stitch. Outline all in split stitch.

STEP 16: PETAL

Outline the petal with split stitch in A3221. Fill the petal with long-and-short stitch, from the outside edge in towards the centre. Fill the petal underside with padded long-and-short stitch. Outline all in split stitch.

STEP 17: PETAL

Outline the petal with split stitch in A3221. Fill the petal with long-and-short stitch, from the outside edge in towards the centre. Fill the petal underside with padded long-and-short stitch. Outline all in split stitch.

PETAL OUTLINES

All petal outlines in D646 or D645.

Step 14
Blanc

Step 14
Blanc, A4096,
A4104, A3221, A3222,
A3712, A3442

Step 16
Blanc, A3442, A3221,
A4096, A4104

Step 16
Blanc, A3222

Step 15
A3442, A3843,
A3842, A3221

Step 15
Blanc, A4104,
A3224, D645

Step 17
Blanc, A4096,
A4104, A3221,
A3222, A3712,
A3442; outline
D645

Step 17
A3221, A3222

STEP 18: PETAL

Outline the petal with split stitch in A3221. Fill the petal with long-and-short stitch, from the outside edge in towards the centre. Outline in split stitch.

STEP 19: PETAL

Outline the petal with split stitch in A3221. Fill the inside of the petal with long-and-short stitch, from the outside edge in towards the centre. Fill the outer edge and turnover with long-and-short stitch. Outline in split stitch.

STEP 20: PETAL

Outline the petal with split stitch in A3221. Fill the petal with long-and-short stitch, from the outside edge in towards the centre. Fill the turnover with padded satin stitch. Outline in split stitch.

STEP 21: PETAL

Outline the petal with split stitch in A3221. Fill the underside of the petal with long-and-short stitch, from the wider edge in towards the centre. Fill the main part with long-and-short stitch. Fill the turnover with padded satin stitch. Outline in split stitch.

STEP 22: PETAL

Outline the petal with split stitch in A3221. Fill the petal with long-and-short stitch, from the outside edge in towards the centre. Outline in split stitch.

STEP 23: PETAL

Outline the petal with split stitch in A3221. Fill the petal with long-and-short stitch, from the outside edge in towards the centre. Outline in split stitch.

PETAL OUTLINES

All petal outlines in D646 or D645.

Step 18
Blanc, A4104, A3221

Step 22
Blanc, A4102, A4104,
A3222, A3442

Step 23
A3222, A3442

Step 21
Blanc, A4104,
A3221, A3222,
A3442

Step 23
Blanc, A4102, A4104, A3222, A3442

Step 23
Blanc, A4096, A3221, A3222, A3442,
A3224, A3712

Step 20
Blanc, A3221, A3222, A3442,
A3224, A4104

Step 20
Blanc, A3221, A3222

Step 19
Blanc, A4096, A3221, A3222,
A3842, A3224, A3712, A3713;
shadows D3787, D645

Step 19
Blanc, A4096, A3221

Step 19
A3221, A3842, A3843, A3844, A4104

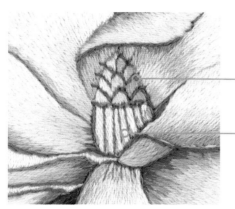

A531, A2232, A3814; outline D646

Blanc; outline D645

STEP 24: FLOWER CENTRE
Fill each segment with padded satin stitch. Outline each with split stitch. Fill the bottom section with straight stitches. Add a line between each in split stitch.

POPPY SAMPLER

PAPAVER SOMNIFERUM

Coloured plate from *Köhler's Medizinal-Pflanzen*, Vol. 2, 1887, from the Kew Art Collection.

PREPARATION

- Transfer the outline to the fabric (see pages 16 and 175).
- Mount your fabric in the hoop (see page 17).
- Follow the step-by-step instructions on pages 156–162.

PROJECT SIZE

14 x 18cm (5½ x 7in)

YOU WILL NEED

- Piece of fabric, 32 x 32cm (12½ x 12½in)
- Threads as per list, opposite
- Super grip or stretcher hoop, size 25.5cm (10in)

Actual size

THREAD LIST

DMC
Prefaced with a 'D' in the steps.
- 10
- 469
- 471
- 472
- 611
- 612
- 613
- 642
- 644
- 733
- 734
- 760
- 830
- 831
- 833
- 834
- 934
- 935
- 936
- 3011
- 3012
- 3013
- 3021
- 3022
- 3023
- 3024
- 3047
- 3052
- 3053
- 3363
- 3371
- 3781
- 3787
- 3827
- 3866

AVÀS Soie D'Alger Silk
Prefaced with an 'A' in the steps.
- 643
- 915
- 916
- 922
- 923
- 2613
- 2643
- 2644
- 2645
- 2646
- 2912
- 4102
- 017f

It is recommended that you use the Au Ver à Soie, Soie D'Alger silk as stated for this project, but if you have difficulty obtaining it, substitute it with DMC by using the conversion chart on page 163 – please note that the results will not be exactly the same.

ORDER OF WORK

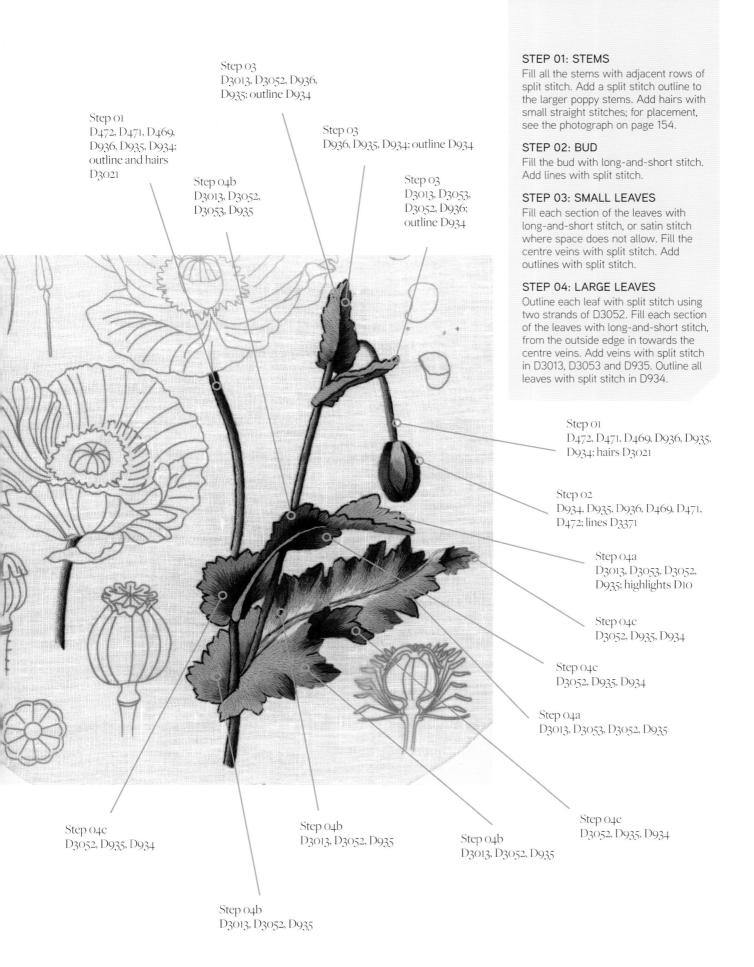

Step 03
D3013, D3052, D936,
D935; outline D934

Step 01
D472, D471, D469,
D936, D935, D934;
outline and hairs
D3021

Step 03
D936, D935, D934; outline D934

Step 04b
D3013, D3052,
D3053, D935

Step 03
D3013, D3053,
D3052, D936;
outline D934

STEP 01: STEMS
Fill all the stems with adjacent rows of
split stitch. Add a split stitch outline to
the larger poppy stems. Add hairs with
small straight stitches; for placement,
see the photograph on page 154.

STEP 02: BUD
Fill the bud with long-and-short stitch.
Add lines with split stitch.

STEP 03: SMALL LEAVES
Fill each section of the leaves with
long-and-short stitch, or satin stitch
where space does not allow. Fill the
centre veins with split stitch. Add
outlines with split stitch.

STEP 04: LARGE LEAVES
Outline each leaf with split stitch using
two strands of D3052. Fill each section
of the leaves with long-and-short stitch,
from the outside edge in towards the
centre veins. Add veins with split stitch
in D3013, D3053 and D935. Outline all
leaves with split stitch in D934.

Step 01
D472, D471, D469, D936, D935,
D934; hairs D3021

Step 02
D934, D935, D936, D469, D471,
D472; lines D3371

Step 04a
D3013, D3053, D3052,
D935; highlights D10

Step 04c
D3052, D935, D934

Step 04c
D3052, D935, D934

Step 04a
D3013, D3053, D3052, D935

Step 04c
D3052, D935, D934

Step 04c
D3052, D935, D934

Step 04b
D3013, D3052, D935

Step 04b
D3013, D3052, D935

Step 04b
D3013, D3052, D935

STEP 05: RED POPPY

Outline all petals with split stitch in two strands of A915. Fill each petal with long-and-short stitch, from the outside edge in towards the centre. Add crease lines in split stitch in a darker shade using the photograph as a guide. Add outlines in split stitch in D3021.

5b. Add straight lines – use the photograph as a guide to the placement of the colours.

5j. Fill each section with long-and-short stitch. Add the lines and outline in split stitch.

5k. Add straight lines around the flower centre. On top of this add French knots using one strand and two twists.

Step 05j
D834, D833, D469, D935; outlines D935

Step 05k
Lines D3781 and D612; French knots D613, D834 and D3781; lines D613, D3781

Step 05c
A922, A923, A915, A916, A2645, A2646

Step 05a
A922, A923, A915, A916, A2645, A2646

Step 05g
A2646, A2645, A2644, A916, A915; turnover A923, A922

Step 05b
A643, D2613, D612, D611; shadows D3781

Step 05d
A922, A923, A2643, A2644

Step 05e
A923, A915, A2645

Step 05h
A922, A923, A916, A2645, A2646

Step 05i
A922, A923, A915, A916, A2644, A2645, A2646

Step 05f
A923, A915, A2645, A2646; turnover A922, A923, A915

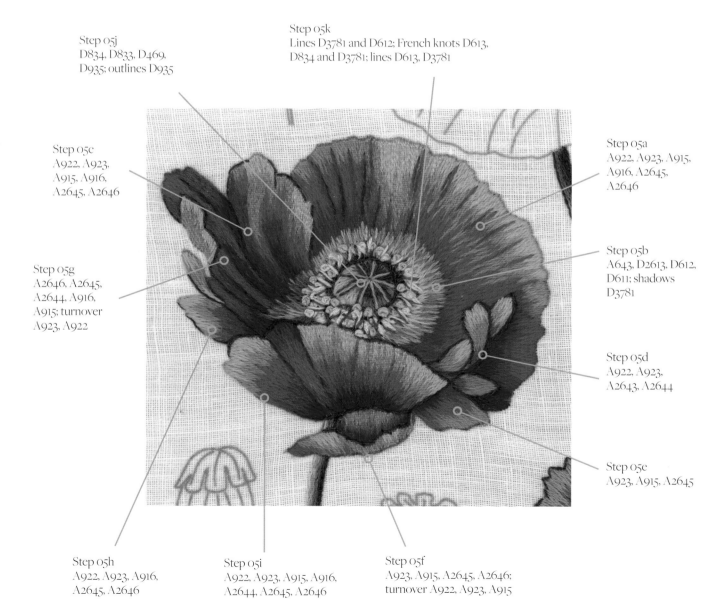

STEP 06

6a. Fill each section with long-and-short stitch. Add lines with split stitch in D3021.
6b. Fill the stem with long-and-short stitch. Add outlines with split stitch.
6c. Fill each section with adjacent rows of split stitch and the outer edge in straight stitches. Add all outlines in split stitch or straight stitches.

Step 06c
D3827, D3047, D612; outlines D3021

Step 06a
D3047, D834, D733; outline D3021

Step 06b
D3047, D834, D733, D831, D830, D3781; outline D3021

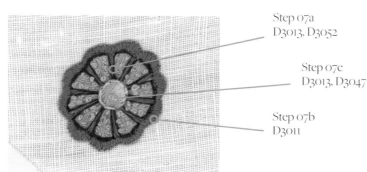

Step 07a
D3013, D3052

Step 07c
D3013, D3047

Step 07b
D3011

STEP 07

7a. Fill with long-and-short stitch in D3052. Add small French knots (one twist) in D3013.
7b. Fill with overcast stitch.
7c. Fill with satin stitch in D3013; outline in D3047. Add all outlines in split stitch D934.

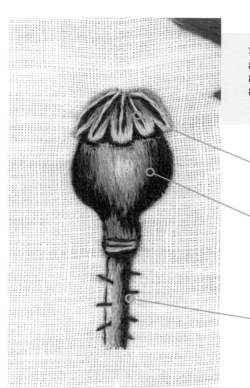

STEP 08

8a. Fill with long-and-short stitch. Add the outline with split stitch.
8b. Fill with adjacent rows of split stitch. Add hairs in straight stitches.
8c. Fill each section with long-and-short stitch. Add lines in split stitch.

Step 08c
D3047, D3053, D3363, D935; lines D3021

Step 08a
D3047, D3013, D3053, D3363, D935, D934; outlines D3021

Step 08b
D3047, D734, D3012, D935; hairs D3021

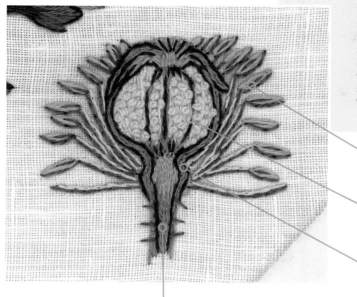

STEP 09

9a. Fill the stem with long-and-short stitch.
9b. Fill the centre with long-and-short stitch. On top of this add French knots using one strand and two twists. Add all outlines in split stitch.
9c. Fill each stem with split stitch. Fill each seed with straight stitches – add a line down the centre in D3787.
9d. Fill with adjacent rows of split stitch.

Step 09c
Stems D3787, D3047; seeds D734; outline D3787

Step 09b
D613; knots D3047; outlines D3021

Step 09d
D3012; hairs D3787

Step 09a
D3053, D3363

STEP 10

10a. Fill with satin stitch in D644. Add French knots on top in D3866, D642 and D3787. Add outlines with split stitch.
10b. Fill with long-and-short stitch; outline in split stitch.
10c. Fill the centre with satin stitch in D3866. Fill the outer area with satin stitch in D642. Add French knots on top in D644 and D3787.
All outlines in split stitch in D3787.

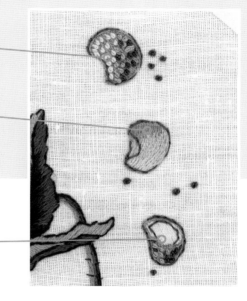

Step 10a
D3866, D644, D642, D3787

Step 10b
D644, D642, D3787

Step 10c
D3866, D644, D642, D3787

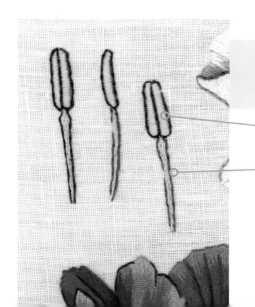

STEP 11

11a. Fill with satin stitch; outline in split stitch.
11b. Fill with adjacent rows of split stitch; outline in split stitch in D3787 or D3021.

Step 11a
D3047, D3021

Step 11b
D613, D3787

STEP 12: WHITE POPPY

12a. Outline each petal in split stitch using two strands of A017f. Fill each petal with long-and-short stitch, from the outside edge in towards the centre. Add lines, shadows and outlines in split stitch.

12b. Fill with long-and-short stitch; outline in split stitch.

12c. Fill each section with long-and-short stitch. Add lines in split stitch.

12d. Add straight lines around the flower centre, working from dark to light.

Step 12a
A4102, A017f, A2912
D760, D3024, D3023, D3022;
lines and shadows in D3787

Step 12c
D734, D3011; lines D935

Step 12b
D734, D3012, D3011; outline D935

Step 12d
D3781, D612, D834, D613

THREAD SUBSTITUTES

Please be aware that it is not possible to provide exact colour matches, so if you choose to use substitutes, your embroidery will invariably look different from the original. Some shades of Au Ver À Soie are not available in the DMC range, so I have chosen the nearest shade so, in some cases, the same colour will have to be repeated.

SPIDER CHRYSANTHEMUM

AVÀS	DMC
1832	164
1833	989
1842	524
1843	523
1844	522
1845	520
2122	3348
2132	471
2133	3347
2134	3346
2135	3345
2926	777
2941	761
3011	760
3733	3011
3734	3012
4147	818
4622	3833
4623	3832
4624	3831

IRIS

AVÀS	DMC
112	828
242	15
532	445
1341	211
1342	155
1343	3746
1344	333
1345	791
1426	939
1721	3761
1842	524
1843	523
1844	522
1845	520
1846	500
2132	471
2133	3347
2134	3346
2135	3345
3732	3013
3733	3012
3734	3011
4213	3776
4214	400
4913	793
4914	792
4915	158
4916	791

MAGNOLIA

AVÀS	DMC
531	3047
2232	3046
3221	01
3222	03
3224	04
3421	644
3442	04
3712	10
3713	3013
3814	3045
3832	372
3841	02
3842	02
3843	03
3844	04
3845	535
3846	535
4096	3865
4102	Ecru
4104	822
Blanc	Blanc

WATERLILY

AVÀS	DMC
2133	3364
3425	501
3426	500
3712	3047
3713	3013
3714	3012
3715	3011
3716	935
3724	3363
3832	613
3833	612
3834	611
3835	610
3836	3781
3841	3024
3843	647
3844	646
3845	645
5022	3813
5023	503
5024	502

RHODODENDRON

AVÀS	DMC
945	816
946	815
1016	321
1831	164
1832	989
1833	988
1834	987
1835	986
1836	895
1843	503
1844	502
1845	501
1846	500
2112	16
2113	471
2114	470
2922	816
2933	3833
2934	3832
2935	3831
2943	3326
3421	524
3422	522
3426	520
4623	3721
4625	3857

POPPY SAMPLER

AVÀS	DMC
643	3825
915	350
916	349
922	352
923	351
2613	922
2643	21
2644	22
2645	3831
2646	815
2912	761
4102	3865
017f	Ecru

THE TEMPLATES

The templates are given here at full size – simply trace them off and transfer them to your fabric using your chosen method.

JAPANESE ANEMONE

see pages 38–43.

FLOWER SAMPLER

see pages 44–93.

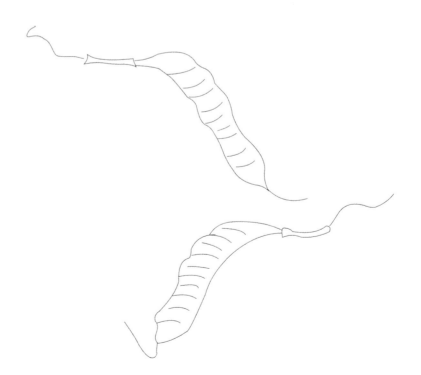

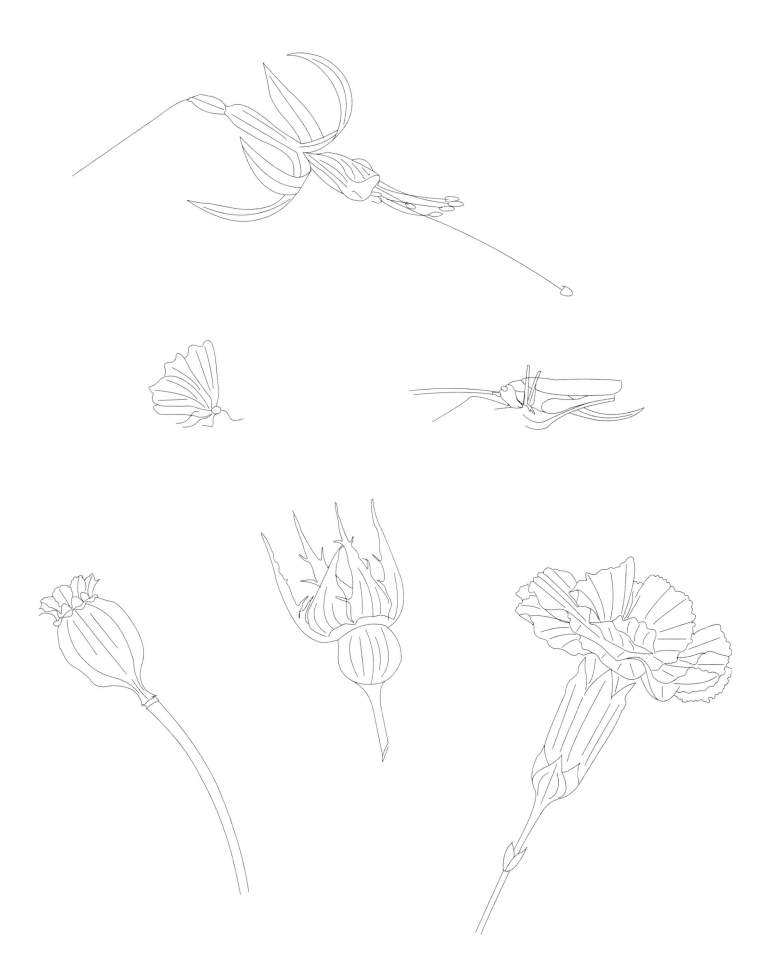

CLEMATIS

see pages 94–99.

CAMELLIA

see pages 100–105.

RHODODENDRON

see pages 108–115.

WATERLILY

see pages 116–121.

IRIS

see pages 122–127.

SPIDER CHRYSANTHEMUM

see pages 128–133.

ROSE

see pages 136–143.

MAGNOLIA

see pages 144–153.

POPPY SAMPLER

see pages 154–162.

USING
IRON-ON
TRANSFERS

This method prevents iron-on transfer paper from slipping while ironing and avoids bleeding lines. Please note that iron-on transfers work best with pure linen or cotton fabric – they will not work on silk fabric.

> **Please note**
> The iron-on transfers are only available with the folder edition of this title.

STEP 1
Set the iron to the hottest dry setting and press the cotton or linen fabric.

STEP 2
Cut out the transfer and place it face up on the ironing mat.

STEP 3
Centre the fabric face-down on top of the transfer and smooth it with your hand so that it lies as flat as possible.

STEP 4
Place the iron on top of the fabric and iron for about one minute. To prevent scorching you can place a piece of parchment paper (baking wrap) on top if you wish.

STEP 5
As you iron you will see the outline being transferred onto the fabric, so you will know when the process is complete.

STEP 6
Here you can see the outline showing through the fabric.

STEP 7
Remove the fabric and turn it over. The print is transferred on the right side of the fabric.

STEP 8
Iron the print one last time to set it. The print is now permanent and ready to stitch.

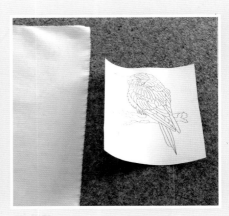